JOB: ORDEAL, DEFIANCE AND HEALING

A Study Guide

by

Zvi A. Yehuda

223.1
Y 35

KRAVITZ MEMORIAL LIBRARY
of Park Synagogue

D0869503

10.00

Copyright © 1990 Hadassah
The Women's Zionist Organization of America, Inc.
All Rights Reserved

90 - 241

Dr. Zvi A. Yehuda is Professor Emeritus of Bible and Rabbinics at the Cleveland College of Jewish Studies and has served as Visiting Professor of Religion at Oberlin College and John Carrol University, Ohio. Ordained in Israel, Rabbi Yehuda received his M.A. and Ph.D. at Yeshiva University, New York. Dr. Yehuda teaches, writes, and lectures on biblical and rabbinic topics, Jewish law, education, ethics and values, and on a wide range of literary, historical, and current issues of Jewish life. He also writes the weekly column "Thought of the Week" for the *Cleveland Jewish News,* and is a Scholar in Residence at the annual Hebrew Week of the Histadruth Ivrith in America, where he delivers lectures in Hebrew on biblical themes.

Dedicated
To The Memory
of My Beloved Son

Ben Zion Yehuda

Who Gave His Life
For Peace In Israel

On
Tu Bishvat, 5735
January 27, 1975

O Earth!
Cover not my blood!
Let no place hide my outcry!

Job 16:18

v

Table of Contents

Foreword

In modern times, when we find it hard to believe in God, the spirit of Job endures.

Judaism instructs us to trust in God and yet at the same time gives us range to challenge him. From Abraham, who demanded that God do justice and not destroy the innocent of Sodom, to Jeremiah and Habakkuk, to Levi Yizhak of Berditchev, who "brought God to trial" because He did little to prevent the suffering of the Jews, the right to challenge God has been a powerful motif in Jewish history.

Despite the attempt of traditionalists to soften the blow of Job's protestations and to view him as patient and long suffering, it cannot be denied that Job's challenge of divine justice brings into question the very meaning and purpose of life. This is what Zvi Yehuda, I believe, is trying so eloquently to say.

Many modern commentators regard Job merely as a mythical figure whose faith remains steadfast despite his ordeals. At the heart of the book, according to Yehuda, is Job's trust, yet defiance, of God. Job never loses faith. Unlike people today, he refuses to become estranged from God. He spurns even his friends, who would blame him for the punishment meted out to him. He neither rebels nor accommodates. Job assumes, instead, the posture of "God arguer" which allows him to withstand and transform his alienation from God. This blending of trust and protest gives meaning to both personal alienation and, in more communal terms, what we Jews call exile.

One of the ironies that shapes this great Jewish book is that its hero is universal. Yet however worldly the book may be, the theme remains a Jewish one. Job protests his situation as an exile by challenging God. His protest leads him from exile into deepened trust. By arguing with God, Job does not augment our sense of estrangement, but helps us to transform our alienation from God and shape from it an image of meaningful existence. Transformation brings healing.

1

The question of trust in life and in God which is at the heart of Job's dialogue with God is equally at the heart of the Jewish people's age-old dialogue with Him. Unlike Albert Camus, who writes in *The Myth of Sysyphus*, "In a universe divested of illusion and light man feels an alien, a stranger, his exile is without remedy since he is deprived of the memory of a lost home or the hope of a promised land," the Jewish people, like Job, refuse to be deprived of the memory of a lost home or the hope of a promised land. That is what makes Job an essential metaphor for our post-Holocaust age, and gives it such majesty and grandeur.

Carol Diament, Ph.D., Editor
June 1990

Preface

This guide to the Book of Job provides a methodological outline for exploring the book's main ideas as they relate to today's world. It is prepared for the reader who is eager to gain new insights into this fascinating book as timeless themes of human suffering, integrity, recovery, friendship, consolation, and the mystery of divine justice are examined. The guide is designed to develop the reader's appreciation of the book as literature as well as his/her critical evaluation of the book's religious and moral lessons.

In particular, the guide is intended for leaders and participants of Bible study groups. It shall prove helpful when used along with the traditional, Masoretic text of Job, in its original or in translation.

There are various translations of the Book of Job, each with its merits and flaws. This guide does not follow any particular translation. All its quotations from the Book of Job, as well as from other biblical and rabbinic sources, are the author's own translations. The guide reflects the author's understanding of the book as a whole, as well as of many of its crucial passages. Intended to stimulate dynamic study of the book and offer a rewarding experience of its intricacy and richness, the guide presents a variety of approaches and interpretations to Job. It can be used in conjunction with any standard commentary or on its own, as preferred by the group. The guide's supplementary chapter (p. 109) will help students in choosing suitable reading material for their study of the Book of Job.

The guide comprises ten chapters which offer ten major themes for study. The first four introduce the book (1), the hero (2), the plot (3), and the issues (4). The fourth chapter also introduces the concept of the "Triangle of Trials and Interactions" of the three parties in the book (Job, God, Job's friends), which is pivotal to the guide's outlook and methodology (p. 39). The subsequent three chapters deal with these three parties on trial: Job (5), God (6), and Job's friends (7). The final three topics in the guide are: Job's recovery (8), Job and the

3

Holocaust (9), and lessons from the Book of Job (10). A supplementary chapter deals with bibliographic data.

To facilitate its utilization by the study group, the guide provides two further didactic aids. Each chapter includes special readings — mostly from the rich selections in *The Dimensions of Job*, edited by Nahum N. Glatzer, which is a required sourcebook and can be obtained through the Hadassah Book Order Service, 5 West 30th Street, New York, NY 10001 — as well as a list of questions for discussion. Both the readings and the discussion questions are presented as educational models to direct and encourage the group's creativity. Readings other than *Dimensions*, listed at the beginning of each chapter, can be duplicated and distributed to the group for analysis in advance of each meeting. These should be chosen at the discretion of the leader.

Hadassah's Jewish Education Department is committed to peer-led study. The group can choose one leader or five or ten, depending on how many assignments any person participating is willing to assume. The guide speaks for itself. With courage and confidence anyone in the group can volunteer to lead. The teacher always learns more than the student. This is the ultimate reward.

I am indebted to many dear friends, colleagues, and students for their support and inspiration in preparing this guide. In particular, I offer my heartfelt thanks to Dr. Carol Diament for her exceptional skill and sensitivity in editing my manuscript; to Sue Mizrahi and Ruth G. Cole for their help and encouragement; to Doris Oxenhorn, Claudia Chernov, Rose Oved Binder, and Leora Tanenbaum for editing and assembling the manuscript for publication; and to Martin Tanenbaum, who called the attention of Hadassah's Jewish Education Department to the Peanuts cartoon (page 106) and provided much insight. Finally, I wish to express my deep gratitude to my family for displaying the proverbial "Jobian patience" with me, and to my dear wife Hassia, for lovingly enduring my full-year preoccupation with Job.

Zvi A. Yehuda

◆ ◆ ◆

Chapter One

The Book Of Job
Within The Context Of Biblical Literature

Required and Suggested Readings

Text (required):

Become acquainted or reacquainted with Job through a cursory, overall reading of the book. Try to get a general and immediate sense of the book as a whole by browsing through its passages. Check the book's beginning (1-4), end (40-42), Job's outburst (3), and soliloquies (27-31), and other parts which draw your attention or spark your curiosity. Don't despair when some (or many) verses and passages appear obscure at first glance. You will further explore them in the course of your study. Once you have read the above, re-read chapters 27-31 in particular. Also take a general look at Ecclesiastes and Proverbs.

Supplementary Readings (suggested):

Leo Baeck, "Job and Kohelet: Books of Wisdom," in *The Dimensions of Job*, edited by Nahum N. Glatzer (New York: Schocken, 1969 [hereinafter cited as *Dimensions*]), pp. 51-56.

Nahum N. Glatzer, "Introduction: A Study of Job," in *Dimensions*, pp. 1-48.

Robert Lowth, "Of the Poem of Job," in *Dimensions*, pp. 132-140.

James B. Pritchard (ed.), *Ancient Near Eastern Texts* (New Jersey: Princeton University Press, 1955), pp. 438ff. and 495ff.

Leslie Fiedler, "Job," in *Congregation: Contemporary Writers Read the Jewish Bible*, edited by David Rosenberg (New York: Harcourt, 1987), pp. 331-345.

Moshe Greenberg, "Job," in *The Literary Guide to the Bible*, edited by Robert Alter and Frank Kermode (Cambridge: Harvard University Press, 1987), pp. 283-304.

Robert Frost, *A Masque of Reason* (New York: Holt, 1945). This intriguing treatment of Job can be obtained in a complete collection of Robert Frost's (1874-1963) poetry.

The Book's Uniqueness

The Book of Job — one of the sacred books of Hebrew Scriptures (*Tanakh*)[1] — is unique in the literature of antiquity. Neither prophetic nor historic, it excels as an extraordinary masterpiece of fictional and philosophical poetry. It is neither epic, dramatic, lyric, nor didactic. Yet, in its wide range of emotion and insight, framed in verses of rare beauty, it embraces something of each of these literary genres. The Book of Job is generally considered to be part of Wisdom literature, which together with Proverbs (*Mishlei*) and Ecclesiastes (*Kohelet*) make up the "trilogy" of Wisdom books.

Biblical Literature: Prophecy, Psalmody, Wisdom

In Jewish tradition, Hebrew Scriptures (*Tanakh*) are divided into three collections of books: Torah (Teaching), *Neviim* (Prophets), and *Ketuvim* (Other Writings).[2] Biblical literature may be divided into three main literary modes: Prophecy, Psalmody, and Wisdom.

Prophecy comprises the books of Torah and *Neviim,* which contain all the biblically recorded words of the prophets. These words are presented as divine revelation ("Thus said the Lord"). Psalmody refers to the biblical liturgic poetry, compiled mostly in the book of Psalms. Wisdom — the literary product of the *hokhmah* schools (of the *hakhamim,* the wise) — comprises three biblical books: Ecclesiastes (*Kohelet*), Proverbs (*Mishlei*), and Job (*Iyyov*). Psalmodic and Wisdom books are part of *Ketuvim.*

Viewed in terms of a divine-human dialogue: Prophecy is God's word to humankind; Psalmody is humanity's response to God; Wisdom is the human response to humanity.

Ecclesiastes, Proverbs, and Job share basic Wisdom traits, yet are different from one another. Ecclesiastes is a book of personal speculations; Proverbs is a collection of educational maxims; Job is a spoken drama, bursting with polemic orations, set within a fictional narrative framework.

The author of Ecclesiastes (Kohelet ben David) appears to be reflective, while the author of Proverbs (Shelomo ben David) speaks as a pragmatist-teacher. Traditionally, both books, as well as Song of Songs (*Shir Ha-Shirim*), are attributed to King Solomon, son of David. The anonymous author of Job focuses on his hero, Job, the pious sufferer. The reader is led to feel that the author identifies completely with Job.

Each of the three Wisdom books — Ecclesiastes, Job, Proverbs — is unique in trend and style. Together they represent three stages of human intellectual deliberation: reflection (Ecclesiastes), disputation (Job), and instruction (Proverbs).

Ecclesiastes is reflective, marked by inconsistencies and contradictions; the sage mostly speaks to himself. Job is an elaborate drama, charged with lament and disputation; the colleagues painfully argue with one another. Proverbs is a collection of incisive, instructional sayings; the teacher addresses his students.

The Book of Job stands in striking contrast to the other two biblical Wisdom books; it is neither dogmatic, like Proverbs, nor nihilistic nor hedonistic, like Ecclesiastes. In many ways, Job can serve as a powerful literary critique of both—assailing the conventional simplicity and certainty of Proverbs, and challenging the spiritual detachment of Ecclesiastes.

The Book of Job — in its religious fervor, sublime poetry, dynamic expression, range of ideas, and depth of psychological insights — is *sui generis*. Because Job is so unusual, biblical scholars have long debated the question of Job's classification.[3] The book's inherent Wisdom qualities, however, are compelling reasons to classify Job as biblical Wisdom literature.

The Three Wisdom Qualities as Reflected in the Book of Job

What are the qualities of biblical Wisdom literature which are found in the Book of Job? In contrast to prophetic and psalmodic literature, biblical Wisdom literature is distinguished by the following three qualities: (1) Rationalism, contemplative and non-revelational; (2) Humanism, focusing on people; (3) Universalism, non-nationalistic.

(1) *Biblical Wisdom is Rationalistic:* It is based on human reason and inquiry, without particular reference to divine revelation. This is crucial in understanding both the plot and orations in the Book of Job. Viewed as non-prophetic, its heavenly scenes and divine revelations must be taken, contextually, as metaphor.

(2) *Biblical Wisdom is Humanistic:* It centers on the human personality, human experience, human destiny, and human sensitivity. Despite its ostensible preoccupation with God, it is intrinsically more concerned with human life and individual freedom and comfort.

The devotional ideals of a transcendent religion are secondary. Wisdom's main objective is human success rather than divine glory.

The prime purpose of the book is not the vindication of God, the adoration of His glory, or the proclamation of His supremacy, but the vindication of Job — the innocent victim of God's testing. Job remains resolute and heroic in his relentless demand for justice from God.

The Jobian drama is cast in irony. While its protagonists try — unsuccessfully! — to justify God, the readers are aware from the start that the real issue is not the justification of God, but the vindication of Job, a human being. The actors may engage in theodicy, but the drama's true concern is anthropodicy.

(3) *Biblical Wisdom is Universal:* In scope and theme, content and form, literary detail, and style of deliberation, biblical Wisdom reflects no Jewish particularity. The biblical books of Wisdom contain no direct or indirect reference to the Jewish people. In contrast to the books of Prophecy and Psalmody, the Wisdom books refer neither to Israel's history nor to its religion. These Hebrew Wisdom books remind us of no Jewish events, heroes, or territories; nor do they recall Jewish symbols, rituals, or festivals.

Rooted in ancient international and Near Eastern culture, biblical Wisdom is openly cosmopolitan, even while it is garbed in Hebraic letters and ideas. It is only in the moral ideas and creative spirit of biblical Wisdom that we detect its uniquely Jewish genius. Job the hero is not Jewish; Job the book is!

Modern scholars have found some vague parallels to Jobian themes in the recently rediscovered texts from the lost literatures of antiquity.[4] Two examples may be mentioned: A Babylonian debate on theodicy between a sufferer and his friends and an Egyptian dispute over suicide.[5] Unlike these long-forgotten ancient texts, the biblical Job has been cherished as a living literature of a living people, exerting its enduring impact on humanity.[6]

The Structure of the Book of Job

The enigmatic structure of the Book of Job is the most vital clue to the book's interpretation. The entire Jobian drama, with its plots and orations, fits into a narrative framework — a prologue (1-2) and an epilogue (42:7-17). Within this fantastic framework, styled in lucid and precise prose, the author enshrines the book's poetry with its rich and powerful verses. This magnificent treasure of poetry contains four parts:

(1) Dialogues between Job and his three friends, which are triggered by Job's initial outburst of curses (3-26);

(2) Job's two soliloquies (27-28; 29-31);

(3) More speeches by a young sage, Elihu (32-37);

(4) Job's encounter with God (38:1-42:6).

Table 1:
Structure of the Book of Job

PROLOGUE	Narrator	1-2		
		CYCLE I	**CYCLE II**	**CYCLE III**
DIALOGUES OF JOB WITH HIS THREE FRIENDS	Job's outburst	3		
	Eliphaz	4-5	15	22
	Job	6-7	16-17	23-24
	Bildad	8	18	25
	Job	9-10	19	26
	Zophar	11	20	—
	Job	12-13-14	21	—
JOB'S TWO SOLILOQUIES	Job	27/28	29/30/31	
YOUNG SAGE'S SPEECHES	Elihu	32-33	34	35 36-37
ENCOUNTER WITH GOD	God	38-39	40:1-2	40:6-41:26
	Job	—	40:3-5	42:1-6
EPILOGUE	Narrator	42:7-17		

What role does the prose narrative play within the Jobian drama as a whole? Does it merely serve as a decorative, legendary framework to the sublime verses of the book, or are the prose parts, the prologue and epilogue, intrinsic elements of the entire poem?

The frame narrative is vital. It makes fundamental points about Job's suffering, and adds to the intrigue and suspense of the drama as well as to the intricacy and depth of the book's religious meaning.

The unique structure of the book is the key to unlocking its hidden meanings. We must approach the book and try to understand it as it is, without attempting to make it conform to our sense of literary order and symmetry. To amend the book is to violate it.

The Story of Job: A Preliminary Briefing

The Book of Job tells the story of a kind and prosperous man who suddenly suffers unmitigated disaster. Job loses his children and property and is afflicted with a loathsome skin disease. How do Job (the sufferer), his society (the consoling friends), and God (Master of the universe), react to all this suffering? This triadic modality in the drama's scope and gestalt — Job/God/Friends — will be elucidated as the tale unfolds.[7]

In the prologue (1-2), Job's suffering is projected as a test of his true piety, to see whether he, in his distress, will continue to cling to his faith in God. In the three poetic cycles of dialogue which follow (3-26), Job's friends explain his suffering as divine retribution for his wrongdoings ("sins"). But Job protests such cruel and undeserved punishment by God, and boldly persists in seeking out the meaning of his suffering.

The next two soliloquies (27-28; 29-31) are milder and more introspective. In the first, Job declares his integrity and his trust in God's ultimate justice (27), and recites a splendid poem in praise of divine Wisdom (28). In the second soliloquy, Job recalls his glorious past (29), portrays his miserable present (30), and asserts his innocence, listing some of his outstanding moral virtues (31).

At this point the drama is interrupted by an unexpected participant, a young, energetic, outspoken philosopher, Elihu, who delivers four lengthy orations (32-33, 34, 35, 36-37). "Full of words," Elihu requires four speeches rather than the customary three. His appearance paves the way for God's final revelation. Elihu's theological contribution to the unresolved debate seems to be that human suffering, in itself, might operate as a form of divine revelation and instruction. God is speaking to the individual sufferer, through his/her pain and agony, with the aim of stirring repentance. Elihu's thesis receives no response.

At last the drama reaches its climax: God's revelation to Job and Job's response (38:1-42:6). God "out of the whirlwind" assails Job with three successive speeches (38-39; 40:1-2; 40:6-41:26). The divine pronouncements overwhelm Job with the grandeur of God's power and wisdom.

In these orations, God does not relate at all to Job's suffering, nor does He directly address any of Job's questions.

Following God's revelation, Job appears silenced. He does not respond to God's first oration and his responses to the last two (40:3-5; 42:1-6) are oblique. Does Job finally submit? If he does, is it out of intimidation or conviction?

In the prose epilogue, which closes the narrative framework of the Jobian drama (42:7-17), God rebukes the friends and indirectly approves of Job's defiance.[8] Then, in an ironic, superficial ending, He restores Job's fortunes. God increases Job's wealth and provides him with new children, including three of the most beautiful daughters. A schematic coupling, the restitution of lost property and the heartless replacement of lost lives, is the symmetrical ending to the book.

This unexpected, shallow ending — which contains no direct response to Job's anguished quest for the meaning of his suffering — has been troubling readers through the centuries.

It seems that in closing the drama neatly, almost derisively, the author is being intentionally sardonic. Perhaps he seeks to demonstrate the absurdity of an easy solution to the Jobian problem.

In a brilliant flash of satire, the narrator remarks (42:15) that "there were no beautiful women in the whole earth like Job's (new) daughters...." This echoes God's words in the prologue, extolling Job's virtue (1:8), that "there is no one like him in the whole earth." The virtue of Job and the beauty of his daughters are matchless. The reader wonders whether the incomparable beauty of Job's newly begotten daughters is an adequate compensation for God's violation of Job, the man of incomparable virtue.

The end of the story now brings us back to the hero in the prologue. Job's misery was triggered not by his misconduct, but by his piety. And precisely because of his unparalleled virtue, Job has been singled out by God to become the target of His boasts, tests, and torments.

Discussion Questions:

1. What draws you to the Book of Job? What do you expect to find in it or learn from it? Attempt to clarify, verbalize, and then write down your present preconceived notions about the book, its hero, its

message, or purpose. Keep your notes for later reference. You will then be able to compare these notes with what you learn during the study sessions, and appreciate the new insights you gain from your study.

2. What are your present expectations from the study of Job? Which do you anticipate the most: to learn more about the Hebrew Bible, study theology, explore human nature, understand the ways of God, penetrate the mystery of evil and suffering, or enjoy great literature? Which is the most dominant factor in convincing you to join the study group on Job?

3. Scholars debate whether the Book of Job should be classified as Wisdom literature. What is your opinion? Why should it? Why should it not?

4. What is your definition of wisdom? How do you distinguish between science, knowledge, understanding, intelligence in modern terms, and "Wisdom" (*hokhmah*) in the biblical sense? Explain your position by pointing to concrete examples.

5. What are the unique features of biblical Wisdom literature? Explain and illustrate.

6. The biblical Wisdom trilogy comprises Job, Proverbs, and Ecclesiastes. Compare and explain the general distinctions between these three books.

7. Do you think that this ancient, biblical Wisdom is still relevant for our complex world? If you think it is, show how it is relevant; if you think it is not, explain why. Conduct a debate; state and argue your opinion.

8. Compare and contrast Fiedler's, Greenberg's, and Frost's treatments of the Book of Job, listed in the supplementary readings to this chapter (p. 5). (Your library or Jewish bookstore should have a copy of *Congregation*, edited by David Rosenberg, and *The Literary Guide to the Bible*, edited by Robert Alter and Frank Kermode. Robert Frost's *A Masque of Reason* is easily accessible; ask your local librarian.)

Notes

1. Tanakh, abbreviation of Torah, *Neviim, Ketuvim*, is the Jewish way of referring to the entire collection of the Hebrew biblical books known in Christianity as "Old Testament." It implies a triadic structure: Torah as distinguished from *Neviim*, and both from *Ketuvim*. The *Tanakh* includes twenty-four books: Five of Torah; eight of *Neviim* (the twelve small booklets of prophecy are compiled as one book, *The Twelve*, meaning, the twelve minor booklets, not "minor Prophets"!); and eleven of *Ketuvim* (*Ezra-Nehemiah* is one book).

2. All three divisions of Hebrew Scriptures comprise Judaism's sacred writings. Torah is often inaccurately rendered as "Law," based on the Greek "*nomos*"; *Ketuvim* means the "miscellany" books, the rest of the writings which are not included in the former two collections.

3. There are scholars who tend to overemphasize Job's departure from the prevailing mood of biblical Wisdom (see Buttenwieser, p. 80; Westermann, p. 1). The predominant view, however, sees the book as belonging to Wisdom (note essays, "Job and Kohelet" by Leo Baeck, and "Job the Righteous Man and Job the Sage" by Yehezkel Kaufmann, in Glatzer's *Dimensions*, pp. 51-56; 65-70).

4. *Ancient Near Eastern Texts* [abbreviated ANET], edited by James B. Pritchard (New Jersey: Princeton University Press, 1955).

5. c. 1400-1000 BCE, *ANET* pp. 438-40; c. 2000-1740 BCE, *ANET* pp. 495ff.

6. Job's canonical status — its sanctity as Scripture and inclusion in *Tanakh* — has (suprisingly) never been questioned in rabbinic tradition. Both its author and its date remain unknown. A wide range of dates have been assigned, from the patriarchal age to the post-exilic (Babylonian Talmud, *Bava Batra*, 14b-15b; *Sanhedrin*, 106a; *Sotah*, 11a). Following Yehezkel Kaufmann and Marvin Pope, scholars today opt for an early pre-exilic date.

7. See chapter 4, "The Triangle of Trials and Interactions," p. 39.

8. See chapter 7, "Between God and Job's Friends," p. 66.

◆ ◆ ◆

Chapter Two

The Hero

Required and Suggested Readings

Text (required):

Job's prologue (1-2) and epilogue (42:7-17); chapters 30-31.

Supplementary Readings (suggested):

William Barrett, "The Hebraic Man of Faith," in *Dimensions*, pp. 272-276.
Seton Pollock, "God and a Heretic," in *Dimensions*, pp. 268-272.
Yehezkel Kaufmann, "Job the Righteous Man and Job the Sage," in *Dimensions*, pp. 65-70.
Leon Roth, "Job and Jonah," in *Dimensions*, pp. 71-74.
Paul Weiss, "God, Job, and Evil," in *Dimensions*, pp. 181-193.

Job — "A Man"

> A man was in the land of Uz;
> Job [was] his name.
> The man had been whole and upright;
> God-fearing and avoider of wrongdoing.

Thus the book opens, with the introduction of its hero (1:1): "A man was," existed, lived, resided (*eesh hayah*). The second half of the verse starts with the same two Hebrew words in reverse: "the man had been" (*ve-hayah ha-eesh*). The first half presents the hero, his abode ("land of Uz"), and his name (*Iyyov*); the second attests to his integrity and exemplary behavior. The first monosyllable in the Book of Job, however, is *eesh* (man, person). This serves as a literary signal that the focus of attention is a human being: "a man" named Job.

The book certainly deals with God, but Job, the symbol of everyman, is the book's hero. The individual human being, struggling valiantly with his destiny on earth, is the major concern of the Book of Job.

What Are in the Names?

Within the context of the Book of Job, the names of both the country (Uz) and the Hero (*Iyyov*) may be regarded as allegorical and imaginary.[1] Uz implies speculation and deliberation (*eza* is counsel, advice), and *Iyyov* means one who is hated and beloved (*ahov*, to love; *ayov*, to hate). In Hebrew, *oyyev* is an enemy (one who hates and/or is hated), and *ohev* is a friend (one who loves and/or is loved). Job's name, *Iyyov*, may combine both: the target of God's love, perceived as hate; or, one who loves God, but resents being treated by Him as an enemy.

The love/hate motif, characterizing the struggle between Job and God, is dominant throughout the book. Job perceives God as both his friend and enemy, and God's treatment of him as a blend of closeness and hostility; the former gratuitous, the latter unfounded. At the end of the first cycle of the dialogue, Job bitterly questions God (13:23-24):

How many are my iniquities and misdeeds?
My transgressions and failures, let me know!
Why do You hide Your face,
and consider me as an enemy (*oyyev*) of You?

The talmudic sages have already pointed to the alliterative quality of Job's complaint: Are You, God, confusing *Iyyov* (Job) and *oyyev* (enemy)?[2] A careful reading of the book should not neglect the poetic symbolism of Job's name (see 27:7; 33:8-10).

Could it be that the hero and his place of residence might also be regarded as non-metaphorical? Uz might well be a real geographic location in Edom; and *Iyyov*, a name of a known ancient historical or legendary figure.[3] Yet it does seem that Job is fully a fictional, symbolic figure.

Hero of the Book — Nonhistorical, Metaphorical

The story tells us where Job lived, but not when. It assigns a place for Job in order to provide a concrete setting for the unfolding drama, but not a specific time. Why? From the ambiance and details of the narrative, we can sense the background of the patriarchal age. Job is described, like Abraham, as a prominent semi-nomad chief. But the narrator avoids defining Job within a chronological context. He avoids this intentionally to stress that Job is not a historical but a fictional figure. It is misleading to ignore this point and theorize about Job's time and place.

From a literary point of view, the story of Job is projected as an allegorical drama and its hero as a metaphorical figure. The book must be approached with this in mind. The Talmud contrasts the opening verse (1:1), that Job "was" (*hayah*), with the drastic claim that: "Job never was, never had been born (*lo hayah ve lo nivra*); he is just a *mashal* (metaphor)."[4] Job the hero is a symbol; Job the book is a poetic fiction.

Job's Universality

Job has a name; an anonymous hero would be too much of an abstraction in a living drama. But he has no ethnic identity. In contrast to his friends who are named in relation to their ethnic origins, Eliphaz the Temanite, Bildad the Shuhite, Zophar the Naamathite, and Elihu the Buzite, Job is not defined by nationality. He is cosmopolitan, universal. He is neither an Israelite nor an Edomite, neither a Jew nor a Gentile; he is a man ("*eesh*") — representing anyone (man, person) who experiences both travail and triumph.

Job's Uniqueness

Although Job represents everyone, he is still unique. As twice asserted by God (1:8; 2:3): "There is no one like him." Job's excellence is defined in the prologue: "whole, upright, God-fearing, and avoider of wrongdoing" (*tam ve-yashar, yere Elohim ve-sar mera*).

These praises are repeated verbatim — with vigorous refrain — three times. The first is by the narrator, informing the readers (1:1); the second and third, by God, boasting about Job — His loyal adherent (His "*eved*": literally, slave, servant; in context, worshipper, devotee) — to the *satan* (1:8; 2:3): "Have you noticed My devotee Job? For there is no one like him on earth, a man who is whole and upright; God-fearing and avoider of wrongdoing."

This rhythmic repetition is poetically effective. While it creates the impression of a stable personality, it also satirically conveys a sense of complacency. By pointing to Job's constancy in his pre-trial stage, it hints that the dynamic traits in the hero's personality will emerge only as a result of his ordeal.

Job's Integrity: Four Attributes of Human Perfection

The four attributes of Job are interconnected. The root of Job's integrity is conveyed by the first trait "*tam*" (wholehearted, blameless), indicating the primary quality of inner wholeness and honesty. This quality (*tumah*, integrity) is later elaborated in the prologue and in Job's speeches. The same key word is there, repeated three times — by God, by Job's wife, and by Job:

> (1) God proudly says to the *satan* (2:3) that "he [Job] still holds on to his integrity." — *tumato*.

> (2) Job's anonymous wife scolds her husband (2:9): "and you still hold on to your integrity?!" — *tumat'kha*.

> (3) Job earnestly pledges before God in his first soliloquy (27:5): "till I die I will not give up my integrity!" And in his second soliloquy, in his final declaration of innocence (31:6): "Let God know my integrity!" — *tumati*.

The second trait "*yashar*" (upright, straight) refers to conduct resulting from the first character trait. In the same manner, the third quality "*yere Elohim*" (one who fears, reveres, worships God) leads to the fourth "*sar mera*" (one who avoids wrongdoing).

For the author, these four attributes seem to define the ideal in human perfection. There is, however, a problem with the fourth, *sar mera* (avoiding wrongdoing). The more poetic "eschewing evil" as well as the more elegant "shunning evil" are fancy but inaccurate renditions.[5] The Hebrew phrase implies action, not sentiment. Job avoided — "turned away from" — wrongdoing. "Avoiding evil" in the biblical sense implies more than passive omission, not doing what is wrong; it involves active commission, doing what is right.[6]

Job's Treatment of His Servant

Job's piety is eloquently demonstrated in his final declaration of innocence, where he describes some of his acts of goodness in relationship to his fellow human beings (31).

Let us focus now on one of Job's self-declared virtues: "*mishpat avdi*" ("justice to my servant"). In biblical Hebrew, *mishpat* means more than justice; in addition to fairness, it implies compassion and protection (the biblical *shofet* functions primarily as a leader who protects his people from enemies, rather than as a judge in the Western sense). Job's statement illustrates his protective treatment of his *eved* (servant or slave) and also his own rationale for treating him this way (31:13-15):

> Did I ever rebuff *mishpat* toward my servant or maid,
> When they had a claim against me?
> What then would I do when God arises?
> When He calls me to account, what do I answer Him?
> Did not my Maker, who shaped me in the womb, make him?
> Did not *Ehad* [the One God] fashion us in a mother's womb?[7]

Job adheres to the biblical concept of human brotherhood and equality, the doctrine that all human beings, man and woman, rich and poor, ruler and worker, master and slave, are inherently alike, since human beings are created (1) by the same God and (2) by the same biological process — birth.[8]

Job's rhetorical question, "Did I ever rebuff (despise) *mishpat* toward my servant (*avdi*)...?" is charged with irony, as it hints God's relationship to him: Am I not Your "*eved*" (servant, devotee)? Why then do You refuse my *mishpat*?

The concluding verses of Job's soliloquies — asserting his innocence before God — are thus also a subtle accusation against God. Job's final words in the dialogues, about the just treatment of "my *eved*" (he who works for me), invoke God's words in the prologue, calling Job "My *eved*" (he who worships Me). Would God refuse justice toward His *eved*?!

Job's reasoning, however, offers a response to his own accusation. Job and his servant are equals, but Job and God are not! Job and his servant are both created by God, through the same birth process. But as for God and Job — God is the Creator and Job is His creature. God created Job, but Job did not "create" his servant; he only acquired him. Can the relationship between human beings rightly be compared to the relationship between the Creator and His creatures — between God and Job? Is God bound by the same standard of ethics as Job with regard to his servant? This question will continue to haunt the reader throughout the Book of Job.

Discussion Questions:

1. Can a real person be so perfect, morally or religiously, as Job is portrayed in the book's narrative? Can you detect flaws in Job's personality, even as he is depicted in the book's plot, in his words or actions?

2. Compare Job's personality before and after his ordeal. What kind of a person emerges from Job's dialogues, from the way he argues with God and his friends, and from his own declaration of innocence (31)? Does this speech violate the ethics of modesty? Does it not sound like boasting? Compare the prologue with Job's speech. God boasts about Job before the *satan*; then, Job boasts about himself before all. How do you feel about both cases?

3. Paul Weiss (*Dimensions*, p. 184) makes disparaging remarks about Job's personality:

> Job is not a pleasant person, rich or poor, in health or in sickness, with children or without. His answer to his friends was that he was at least as good as any — which he undoubtedly was, except for saying so. He insists, a little too violently, that there is no wickedness in his heart and that his conduct is above reproach.

React to Weiss' critique. Do you agree with him? If you do, elaborate and add examples; if you don't, offer a good defense of Job.

4. What do you make of the verbal exchange between Job and his wife? Explain the behavior of both — the woman's desperate appeal and Job's angry retort.

5. The prologue's formula detailing Job's excellence (thrice repeated) is rendered by Stephen Mitchell, *Into the Whirlwind: A Translation of the Book of Job* (New York: Doubleday, 1979): "He was a thoroughly good man, who feared God and did nothing wrong." In a later edition (San Francisco: North Point Press, 1987), this rendition is modified: "He was a man of perfect integrity, who feared God and avoided evil." Which version do you prefer, and why?

Notes

1. Moses Maimonides, *The Guide for the Perplexed*, translation from the original Arabic by M. Friedlander (New York: Dover, 1956), 3:23, p. 299.

2. Babylonian Talmud, *Bava Batra*, 15b.

3. See Ezekiel 14:14, 14:20.

4. Babylonian Talmud, *Bava Batra*, 15b.

5. The first in the translation of the King James Version (1611); the second in both translations of the Jewish Publication Society (the old, of 1917, and the new, of 1982).

6. Psalms 34:15.

7. The last line can also be rendered: "Did not He [my Maker] fashion us [both me and my servant] in one [*ehad*, identical] womb [*be-rehem*]?" The Hebrew *rehem* implies love and protection (*rahamim* means compassion). The end of the line thus implies: Did not God create all of us with love? Or, within a loving, protective, mother's womb?

8. The dual implication derives from the ambiguity of *ehad*: One [God] or one [womb]? See above *note* 7.

◆ ◆ ◆

Chapter Three

The Plot

Required and Suggested Readings

Text (required):

Prologue (1-2) and epilogue (42:7-17); chapters 3, 32, 38, 40:3-42:6.

Supplementary Readings (suggested):

G.K. Chesterton, "Man is Most Comforted by Paradoxes," in *Dimensions*, pp. 228-237.

James B. Conant, "Job: The Twofold Answer," in *Dimensions*, pp. 247-250.

Marvin H. Pope, "Viewed as a Whole," in *Dimensions*, pp. 276-277.

H. Wheeler Robinson, "Life—A Mystery," in *Dimensions*, pp. 245-246.

The Prologue — Background Setting:
The Concealed Origins of Job's Ordeal

The prologue (1-2), an integral part of the drama, serves as the chorus in Greek tragedy. In five scenes, briefly sketched, it establishes the dramatic situation of the entire book. All the book's details proceed from the prologue. Thus, all the actions and speeches in the book must be understood and evaluated from the vantage point of the prologue. Yet, the content of the prologue, so lucidly presented, is by definition a mystery, a heavenly secret. None among the earthly participants in the Jobian drama is supposed to know or suspect any part of its content.

The prologue, however, reveals the transcendent source of Job's ordeal. Initiated by God in His heavenly court, Job's ordeal is projected as a test of his integrity. It thus offers a possible meaning or explanation to Job's sufferings. This, ironically, is revealed to the readers only, while it remains concealed from all the human protagonists throughout the entire drama.

The single focus of attention in the prologue is on one individual — Job. Job is God-fearing; he is recognized by God as "My devotee" (*avdi*). Although Job is aware of God as the Supreme Master, he is unaware of God's scheming in Heaven. Man on earth knows not the mysteries of Heaven, while God in Heaven knows all. God watches Job, observes his actions and reactions, delights in his human perfection, and takes pride in him. Responding to the *satan's* challenge, God puts Job to the test. Faced with calamity, will Job still maintain his faith in God, or renounce and blaspheme Him? But, as the reader painfully realizes, neither Job nor any other mortal in the drama knows anything about this test. Only the reader knows.

Structure and Content of the Prologue's Scenes

The settings of the five scenes alternate between Earth and Heaven. Three of the five scenes — first, middle, and last — take place on Earth; the other two, in Heaven. The rapid shifts between Heaven and Earth intensify the dramatic tension. The main actor in the earthly scenes is Job, the archetypal individual, yet he is surrounded by family, servants, and friends. The actors in the heavenly scenes, who engage in two fateful dialogues, are two: God and the *satan* (*ha-satan*).

Who is the *Satan*?

"The *satan*" (*ha-satan*, with the definite article) appears only in the two heavenly scenes of the prologue. Otherwise, he is neither mentioned nor hinted at in the rest of the book. Who is he? And what is his role within the context of the story?

Clearly, the *satan* interacts only with God, not with people. Who afflicts Job with his repulsive skin disease? In its crafted Hebrew syntax, "The *satan* departed from the presence of God and inflicted Job" (2:7b) remains ambivalent, letting us wonder who inflicted Job, God or the *satan*. At any rate, the *satan* acts merely as an agent of God.

In biblical Hebrew, *satan* is not a proper name but a title indicating function. Within the context of a human court of law or a mundane royal council, the *satan* is a designated official who serves as the prosecuting attorney, the accuser.[1] He also may have the role of inspecting the provinces under his jurisdiction and reporting to the ruler. The *satan* in the heavenly court seems to be engaged in some sort of surveillance, traversing the earth to check on the lives of human beings.[2]

We must emphasize, at the very start of our study of the Book of Job, that "the *satan*" of the book is not Satan (*sayt'n*) of the English vernacular. The *satan* is a Hebrew noun, spelled with a small *s* and its two vowels pronounced with the Hebrew (*sefardi*) *kamatz* (like "car"). This usage in the spelling and pronunciation of *satan* should be observed by students of the book of Job in order to avoid confusion with the English Satan. It is recommended that within the context of Job we use the phrase "the *satan*" — *italicized* (as a foreign word), uncapitalized, with the definite article (as a common noun), and pronounced with the accent on the last syllable (as in the Hebrew) — in order to distinguish this biblical term from its derivative word, the English Satan.

Nor is the *satan* of the Book of Job equivalent to the devil of later Jewish and Christian traditions; he is not "satanic" — he does not represent nor generate evil. The *satan* of the book is neither diabolic nor demonic. He is not the villain. Neither is he the enemy nor adversary of God nor of humanity. He is simply one of the celestial officers serving the High King, and does not get involved with human beings. He is definitely not the mythical, theological figure, Satan. This misunderstanding of the Jobian *satan* figure, due to anachronistic thinking and Christological impact, is currently pervasive and clouds the reader's ability to appreciate the meaning and lessons of the book or its Hebraic spirit.

The *satan* in the Book of Job does not appear "as the figure of acting and living evil" and does not have "an independent personality" — popular notions to the contrary notwithstanding.[3] In biblical imagery, the *satan* is one of the countless angels (*benei elohim*), celestial messengers, serving God, designated by Him to fulfill His exclusive Will.

The Hebrew biblical *satan* represents neither goodness nor evil. Within the biblical outlook, good and evil (*tov* and *ra*) are a matter of free choice; the *satan* has no choice. Only human beings, made in God's image, are endowed with this gift of free choice; angels are not. The *satan* is God's celestial angel (messenger).

So, what is the *satan's* role in the Book of Job?

A Symbolic Link Between Heaven and Earth: Distance and Interaction Between the Human and Divine Realms

It may well be that the *satan* serves as a symbolic bridge between Heaven and Earth. This can be seen from the *satan's* first answer to God in Heaven, that he has been (1:7) "roaming all over the Earth."

Between Heaven and Earth: The distance as well as the interaction between the two is underlined in the Book of Job. The author may have had in mind the concept of distance between the two realms, the divine and the human, as articulated in biblical Wisdom and Prophecy.[4]

The prologue in the Book of Job illustrates the contrast between Heaven and Earth. As much as Heaven is aware of Earth, the human being on earth will never comprehend the ways and thoughts of Heaven. Still, a mortal person will continue to strive to cling to the divine. Between divinity and humanity, there is both a gap and a bridge. The *satan* in the Book of Job serves as a dramatic symbol illustrating this elusive but potent link between the two worlds — the divine and the human. By treating the Jobian *satan* as "satanic" (demonic, evil), we create a scapegoat for our moral indignation, thus missing the whole point of the Jobian drama. Whoever is to be blamed for evil in the world, for human depravity and misery — God or man, both or neither — it is certainly not the *satan* in the Book of Job!

Three Earthly Scenes: Job's Three Devotional Expressions

Job's religious disposition is reflected in each of the three earthly scenes (first, third, and fifth), by three different expressions of devotion to God: (1) Job's routine devotion, in the pre-trial stage (in the first scene, 1:5); (2) Job's reaction to the first phase of his test (in the third scene, 1:20-22); (3) Job's reaction to the second phase of his test (in the fifth scene, 2:10).

Throughout the year (*kol hayyamim*) Job would offer weekly sacrifices, for each one of his children, to atone for a possible lapse in their faith due to excessive merriment. Job thought: "Perhaps my children have failed, and blasphemed God in their hearts." Job is not worried about possible overt transgressions against God by his children; apparently he knows them to be outwardly observant and devoted to God. But he worries about their state of mind, their attitude to God "in their hearts." The atonement ritual involves the sacrifice of *olot* (burnt offerings), which are totally consumed by sacred fire. This offering, by its name and procedure, indicates spiritual elevation, enthusiasm, and completeness. It atones for flaws in one's attitude and state of mind.

Job is thus portrayed, from the very start, as one who is consistently worried about blaspheming God. This fear, warranted or groundless, haunts Job even in the pre-trial stage when he is depicted as pious and tranquil (compare Job's own statement, 3:25-26). But, tragically, only then. Ironically, after being deprived of his children, he becomes painfully "relieved" of any more worry about their devotional integrity. But now, in the prologue, prior to his own ordeal, Job is concerned with his children's good standing before God.

This subtle, brief episode prepares the reader for the later presumptuous accusation which is unleashed by Bildad against Job (8:4; echoing 1:5):

> If your children failed Him,
> He dispatched them by the grip of their guilt.
> Now, if you yourself will search for God,
> And to the Almighty you will make supplication;
> If you are pure and upright,
> Then He will respond to you,
> And restore your rightful habitation.

In the prologue Job fears blasphemy committed not by himself, but by his children; not openly, but inwardly; not with offensive words, but with irreverent feelings.

The motif of fear of blasphemy is thus projected as early as the first scene of the prologue. But, ironically, the fear in the human sphere is in reverse to that in Heaven. While Job fears that blasphemy — inwardly committed by his sons — will result from their abundant success and excessive rejoicing,[5] the heavenly court fears that blasphemy — committed by Job, verbally and openly — will result from his anguish. Job worries that his sons' affluence will lead to their *impiety*, yet the *satan*, in a diametrically opposite line of reasoning, argues that Job's affluence is the reason for his *piety*, and that in its absence Job will be tempted to blaspheme God.

Thus, during the brief episode in the first scene (1:5), the reader has already been introduced to the fateful question of the interrelationship between religious devotion and material success. Is there any interconnection between a person's conduct — whether one does right or wrong — and a person's lot — whether one meets success or failure? Was Job's ordeal a result of his bad conduct (the friends' view) or, the reverse, his good conduct (the prologue's view)? Will blasphemy be triggered by affluence (Job's view of his sons) or, the opposite, by misery (the *satan*'s view of Job)?

The other two earthly scenes describe Job's reactions to his test; he has a different reaction to each of the test's two phases. In a more profound sense, all of Job's three devotional expressions may be classified as reactive. Even his routine devotion in the first scene can be viewed as Job's reaction to his own fear concerning his sons' true feelings about God.

In a dynamic sequence, all three of Job's devotional expressions in the prologue show us his reactive attitude to God. The reader is moved to wonder: Does Job progress or regress in his devotion to God?

Job's Reaction to the First Phase of His Test

The first phase of Job's ordeal has been limited, by God's explicit order to the *satan* (1:12), to "all that he has," sparing Job himself: "Do not lay your hand on him!" This phrase remarkably echoes the divine voice in the *akedah* story, urging Abraham to spare his son.[6] Ironically, in contrast to the *akedah*, all Job's children (in addition to all his servants) are fair game for destruction. They are sacrificed by God to facilitate His test of Job's piety.

The narrator, however, does not directly describe the events of destruction. More subtly, the narrator makes reference only to the news about them. This is accomplished by a swift succession of messengers to a confounded Job, each of whom is a lone witness and survivor of the reported catastrophic event. They leave him no moment of respite. The reader, like Job, is informed of the tragic occurrences only by the messengers' reports; thus the reader experiences, together with Job, each blow as a thunderbolt from the blue. The reader will now wonder:

> How will Job, the righteous man, react to events, the purpose of which is unknown to him and which, he may deduce according to Wisdom philosophy, constitute a negation of God's righteousness?[7]

How does Job react? First in a mute succession of gestures, then in three Wisdom-liturgical aphorisms (1:20):

> Then Job rose up, tore his robe, shaved his head, fell
> down to the ground, bowed; and said:
> (1) Naked I came out of my mother's womb;
> And naked I shall return there (to dust).[8]
> (2) The Lord has given, the Lord has taken away;
> (3) Blessed is the name of the Lord.

In a profoundly religious mood — after acknowledging (1) his own human futility and (2) God's ultimate mastery — Job utters his blessing (3): "Blessed is the name of the Lord." The narrator concludes with a laudatory verse (1:22): "Despite all this [misfortune], Job did not slip (*hatah*, fail), nor cast reproach on God." This verse, in contrast to the one which concludes the second phase of his test (2:10), is not confined to speech, and thus may imply that even "in his heart" Job did not attribute any fault to God.

Job's Reaction to the Second Phase of His Test

The second phase of Job's test is more severe and Job's reaction, as expected, is less devout. God has given the *satan* a free hand, with only one reservation (2:6): "See, he is all in your hand, only spare his life!" Job's life is spared for the sake of the test if not for his own. Then (2:7), "[he/He] inflicted Job with a severe skin disease, from the sole of his foot to the crown of his head." This cryptic verse does not name the perpetrator. Job holds God responsible; he reacts non-verbally, scratching himself in the midst of the ashes. He neither blesses, as after the first phase, nor blasphemes, as anticipated by the *satan* in the celestial scene and urged by his wife in the terrestrial scene.

If Job does not react verbally to his newly acquired skin disease, he surely reacts so to his wife. She confronts him (2:9): "You still hold on to your integrity? Blaspheme God and die!" Now Job, who is able to stifle his rage against God, lashes out at his wife (2:10). Job displays a thoroughly human trait. Rage withheld emerges at the wrong time, against the wrong person ("displacement" in modern terms). "You talk as any shameless woman might talk! Should we accept from God only the good (*ha-tov*), and not accept the bad (*ha-ra*)?"

Job's response to his wife betrays his bitter resentment upon receiving "the bad" from God. His rhetorical question is devoid of logic. Why not accept only the good and reject the bad, as we usually do in life? Job's awkward retort incorporates a religious position: Both the good and the bad come from God; both are His decrees. As one accepts from God the good, so should one accept the bad. But "accepting" the good is different from "accepting" the bad. The good we gladly welcome; the bad we must endure. What did Job mean by "acceptance" of the bad? Resignation? Surrender? Within the context of Job's story, this acquiescence to God's decree simply means refraining from blasphemy, accepting His "bad" decrees without "cursing" Him. Job passively "accepts" the bad; he neither curses nor blesses (the two antithetical meanings of *barekh*). Does Job, in his later dialogues and soliloquies, really "accept" God's inflictions? Does he, indeed, act in accordance with his sermon to his wife?

At this stage, however, Job remains sitting within his ashes. He does not bow before God, nor rail against Him. The narrator concludes (2:10): "In all this Job did not fail with his lips...." This praise for Job, at the end of the second phase, is clearly more restrained than the one at the end of the first phase. It adds "with his lips" and omits that he did not "cast reproach on God."

A rabbinic conclusion: "With his lips Job did not fail, but in his heart he failed."[9] The irony here is intended. It is, after all, Job who would make atonement for his children's hypothetical failure in their hearts! The narrator, however, does not openly accuse Job of a lapse of faith in his heart. Nor could he do so, for "man sees only what is visible; only God sees into the heart."[10] The narrator is only human.

Now, when bad things happen to Job, he accepts them from God, as he has before accepted the good things, without blasphemy, but also without praise. Job's reaction to the second phase of his test is different from his reaction to the first phase. Earlier, after the loss of all his possessions and children, he was able to recite a blessing ("Blessed is the name of the Lord!"). But now, in his most degrading personal condition, he cannot bring himself to bless God.

Why? Is he more devastated by his skin affliction than by the loss of all his children? The fact remains that while Job is afflicted by his odious skin disease, "from the sole of his foot to the crown of his head," scratching himself, sitting in the ashes — he does not bless God! In this miserable condition which engulfs his entire body, Job withholds his recital of a proper blessing to God. We wonder why. Is it because he has now lost his abiding faith in God? Or is it precisely because he still maintains his profound reverence for God? Job's integrity is splendidly displayed. He would rather remain silent, if he is unable to turn to God with dignity. Job would not say words to God just to please Him, if he does not feel he can say them truthfully. Job did not fail "with his lips" — either by cursing Him or by blessing Him.

Appropriating the Jobian model, the talmudic sages teach:

> In the same way we recite a blessing on the good,
> So do we recite a blessing on the bad.[11]

What does "in the same way" mean? The same intensity of faith, not the same formula of blessing:

> On good tidings one recites:
> "Blessed is the Good One
> who grants goodness" (*Hatov ve-Hametiv*);
> On bad news one recites:
> "Blessed is the Judge of truth" (*Dayan Haemet*).[12]

Rabbinic tradition thus insists that the difference between good happenings and bad, from a purely human perspective, must never be blurred. One must never accept the good happenings as if they are bad, nor accept the bad happenings as if they are good. But one must accept both with the same abiding faith in the ultimate justice of God. In Judaism this belief is called *zidduk ha-din*: the (human) justification of the (divine) verdict. This concept clearly has its roots in Job's different reactions to the two phases of his test.

Two Parallel Inquiries:
Is There Human Integrity? Is There Divine Justice?

The Book of Job deals with two parallel themes: human integrity and divine justice. The former is the focal point of the prologue. Is there such a human virtue as genuine righteousness, acting justly for its own sake and not for reward? The latter, divine justice (theodicy, see end of chapter), is debated in the dialogues. Is there undeserved human suffering? The former inquiry asks whether man is just, the latter whether God is just.

These two themes, human integrity and divine justice, are reciprocal. In the heavenly sphere (of God), man (Job) is tested; in the human sphere, God is judged. To the divine question, related to Job's integrity — Is there human righteousness for its own sake? — God answers "Yes" (1:8; 2:3), and the *satan*, "No" (1:9). To the human question, related to God's justice — Is there innocent suffering? — Job answers "Yes" (9:17), and his friends, "No" (4:7).

The Key Word *"Hinam"* — "For No Reason"

The interconnectedness of the two issues is artistically demonstrated by the use of the Hebrew word *"hinam,"* which in context means "for no reason," that is, without justified cause or purpose, with no expectation of reward (literally, "gratuitously"). The *satan* initiated the use of the term in his provocative report to God (1:9). Subsequently, both God (2:3) and Job (9:17) use the same term to make their points. In the heavenly sphere the two related questions are entwined. The *satan*'s question to God is: "Does Job serve God for no reason (*hinam*)?" God's question to the *satan* is (2:3): "Why did you provoke Me to destroy him for no reason (*hinam*)?"

Unaware of the heavenly dialogue, Job complains that God (9:17) "has multiplied my wounds for no reason (*hinam*)." Ironically, by using the same key word *hinam* when he accuses God of injustice, Job echoes God's concern for justice. Job is asking his friends the same question about God that God was asking the *satan* about Job: Would God inflict suffering for no reason (*hinam*)?

The key word *hinam* — spoken by the *satan*, God, and Job — displays various nuances: (1) by the *satan*, it challenges the integrity of Job; (2) by God, it confirms the integrity of Job; (3) by Job, it challenges the justice of God.

Job insists that there is innocent suffering, and that God wounded him for no reason (*hinam*). The friends are convinced otherwise, that no innocent person suffers; if one does, this proves one is not innocent. The *satan*, aware of Job's splendid record of piety, is not at all convinced that Job's righteousness is genuine. Job is good, so claims the *satan*, only because he enjoys God's goodness and favor. Once Job is outside God's protection, loses his wealth and family, he will curse God to His face. Apparently, the *satan* does not believe that a human being is capable of disinterested righteousness. God, displaying a higher opinion on human potential for goodness, insists otherwise: Job will never renounce God, even in the depths of his affliction.

Job proves God right; God proves Job right. Job proves that his righteousness was unconditional. He did serve God "for no reason." God, in the prologue, confirms Job's argument that indeed the innocent may suffer. All this leads to the fundamental question of reconciling the theory of divine justice with the reality of human suffering — the issue of theodicy.

What is Theodicy?

The overriding issue debated in the dialogues of the Book of Job is that of God's justice. This is known in modern theology by the term "theodicy" (a combination of two Greek words: *theos*, God, and *dike*, justice), namely, the theory that God is just. Theodicy deals with the interpretation and vindication of God's justice. It probes into the most difficult question asked by the ancient prophets of Israel: Why do the innocent suffer and the wicked prosper? How can we reconcile the existence of evil with a world governed by a benevolent God?

We will learn more of the question, and of the different answers suggested as solutions to this question, after being introduced to the issues in the book.[13]

Discussion Questions:

1. By pointing to various examples from the Book of Job and other biblical sources (or world literature), illustrate the sense of identification, as well as tension, that develops between the reader and the character. Consider each of the following situations:

(a) The reader is informed by the narrative, but the characters remain ignorant of this knowledge throughout the entire drama (the heavenly scheme of testing Job);

(b) The reader is informed in the narrative together with the character (1:14);

(c) The characters are unaware of each other's points of view, but the reader has the benefit of knowing both views (Megillat Esther);

(d) The reader remains ignorant of the narrational detail until he/she is informed by the characters' own speeches (Joseph pleads to his brothers and their indifference, Genesis 42:21; the content of Jonah's prophecy to Nineveh, 3:4, and the reason he gives to God for his flight to Tarshish, 4:2).

Reflect on the dramatic impact in each situation and the reasons for employing one particular style in each case.

2. Job's response to his wife is stated in the original Hebrew as a rhetorical question (2:10): "Shall we accept only the good [gifts] from God, and not accept [from Him] the bad [gifts]?" In Stephen Mitchell's translation (1987), this verse is stated affirmatively: "We have accepted good fortune from God; surely we can accept bad fortune too." Is this translation justified? How does this change of style, from the interrogative to the declarative, affect the meaning and impact of Job's original statement?

Notes

1. See Zechariah 3:1-2.

2. *Ibid.*, 1:10-11.

3. As claimed, for example, by Richard E. Singer, *Job's Encounter* (New York: Bookman, 1963), p. 17.

4. See Ecclesiastes 5:1; Isaiah 55:9.

5. See Deuteronomy 32:15; Proverbs 30:9.

6. Genesis 22:12.

7. Meir Weiss, *The Story of Job's Beginning* (Jerusalem: Magnes Press, 1983), p. 57.

8. "There" (*shamah*) is a euphemism for the realm of death, the grave, the dust. Compare Ecclesiastes 5:14 and 9:10: "in *sheol*, to where you go 'there' (*shammah*)." In Job 3:19, "there" (*sham*) refers to the grave. See Genesis 3:19: "For you are dust, and to dust will you return." Metaphorically one returns to the "mother's womb" of all humans, the dust (Genesis 2:7).

9. Babylonian Talmud, *Bava Batra* 16b.

10. I Samuel 16:7.

11. Mishnah, *Berakhot* 9:5.

12. *Ibid.*, 9:1.

13. See chapter 10, "Lessons From the Book of Job," p. 97.

◆ ◆ ◆

Chapter Four

The Issues

Required and Suggested Readings

Text (required):

Prologue (1-2); first and second cycles of dialogues (3-14; 15-21); epilogue (42:7-17).

Supplementary Readings (suggested):

Emil G. Kraeling, "A Theodicy — And More," in *Dimensions*, pp. 205-214.
W.O.E. Oesterley and T.H. Robinson, "The Three Stages of the Book," in *Dimensions*, pp. 214-217.
Rudolf Otto, "The Element of the Mysterious," in *Dimensions*, pp. 225-228.
Stephen Mitchell, *The Book of Job — Translated and with an Introduction* (San Francisco: North Point Press, 1987).[1]

The Prologue — Its Role and Literary Qualities

The prologue, by virtue of the dramatic role it plays, presents esoteric details which are not supposed to be mentioned in the rest of the book. The heavenly scene is a hidden plot — a secret known only to the celestial participants. The *satan*, who plays the critical roles of both instigator and executioner, is completely ignored in the remainder of the book.

The divine plot remains unknown to the book's human protagonists; yet, it is projected beforehand to the book's readers. We, the readers, are privy to the secret scheme of the heavenly tribunal, supposedly the "official" reason for Job's sufferings, which is concealed from the victim and his friends. The fact that the readers of the book know what the actors in the book do not surely adds a special element of tension to the whole story. But, besides the intensification of suspense, this literary device of selective narration — blending revealing (to the readers) with concealing (from the protagonists) — dramatizes the doctrine of the book, that no human being on earth may dare claim knowledge of the divine plan in Heaven. Hidden are the ways of God, as are the reasons for human suffering.

The reason for Job's suffering, as projected in the prologue, is the divine scheme to test Job's integrity. God, in His initial remark to the *satan*, boasts of Job's piety. Challenged by the *satan*, God then enters into a wager with him. God allows for Job's torment in order to prove the veracity of His claim, as well as the authenticity of Job's piety. Now, presumably, we know why Job has been suffering, how he has been singled out by God for this awesome ordeal. But, do we really know?

Intriguingly, the answer is given to us even before the question is raised, and disappears afterwards. It exerts its haunting impact on us, yet lacks the power of conviction and raises further questions. We wonder: Is the heavenly scene a parody? Does it aim to alert the reader that Job's ordeal is undeserved? Is it a hint that human suffering may be viewed as divine testing? We are led to presume that we know the reason for Job's suffering, while throughout the anguished dialogues, stormy revelation, and "happy ending" epilogue, the human actors are left unsuspecting.

Coping With the Book's Moral and Theological Problems

This internal conflict of plot, speech, narration, and oration raises many questions in the minds of the readers, leading to a variety of contradictory conclusions. The most gnawing question, however, is: Do we really know? Is the official reason, given in the prologue, the true one? Does the author really expect us to take his report on the heavenly proceedings, artfully crafted in folktale style, seriously? We wonder: If indeed the wager between God and the *satan* is the reason for Job's torment, why then does God not see fit to mention it or apologize for it? He does not do so either in His final answer to Job "from the whirlwind" (38:1) or at any other appropriate occasion!

The Interpretive Role of the Reader in the Book of Job

Readers, particularly of biblical literature, are expected to be more than passively receptive. They are called upon to become active participants in the creative literary process, to search for deeper levels of interpretation. We, the readers, are given the right to probe further and determine what all this means to us.[2]

In the case of the Book of Job, the story is presented not as history but as metaphor, not as fact but as fiction. Surely, the author does not claim to be a witness to the heavenly proceedings, nor to be prophetically informed about them.

It is important to remember that in Jewish tradition, the Book of Job is included as part of the Writings (*Ketuvim*), not the Prophets (*Neviim*). The book does not claim revelatory authority; it teaches us human wisdom — speculations and imaginings of inspired sages.[3] As Job the hero is fictional, so is Job the book. God's words in the narrative and in His final revelation to Job are merely fiction.[4]

On the literary and conceptual levels, the prologue's fantastic portrayal of the heavenly scenes thus leads to many intriguing concepts. The vivid depiction of the heavenly plot in the prologue, ignored throughout the rest of the book, may be viewed as satire. It illustrates how the sufferer and the "theologians" who comfort him are in the dark when they endeavor to explain human suffering and divine justice.

When Job's friends insist that human suffering is the result of human wickedness, the reader, still under the enchantment of the prologue, may react to the friends' lofty speeches with skepticism, because the reader has been prepared to understand that Job's sufferings are not the result of his vices, but of his unsurpassed perfection. All this, however, remains untold to Job. Job, ignorant of the reason for his ordeal, suffers not only physical pain, but psychological anguish. He persists in asking God, "Why?" — but he gets no answer.

In no verse in the whole book of Job does God appear merciful either in His deeds or words. Yet, ironically, in the wager with the *satan*, He emerges, momentarily, as a caring God, as One who delights and believes in human integrity. God shows complete faith in the goodness of Job. He is proud of Job's perfection. He stages the wager in order to prove His trust in Job's perfect faith. This in itself, however, is a shocking paradox. The caring God becomes a cruel God. In order to prove Job's piety, He toys with Job's life. The solicitous God crushes His pious devotee, of whom He is so proud! At the end, God overwhelms Job, but does not console him. God never addresses Job's earnest quest to know: "Why do I suffer?"

"Revealing" the Meaning of Suffering: Does It Offer Any Comfort to the Sufferer?

Does a sufferer derive any comfort from knowing the reason for his or her suffering? Let us say the sufferer is told that suffering is a divine punishment for wickedness (retributive), or that it is a divine call for improvement (instructive). Then, what? These explanations may, perhaps, provide the sufferer with a ray of hope; the person will resolve to repent, improve, mend his or her ways, and then expect to be restored. But, on the other hand, these kinds of explanations may add insult to injury, burden the sufferer with additional guilt or frustration. The prologue explains Job's suffering neither as punitive (as the friends do) nor as instructive (as Elihu does), but rather as explorative — a divine test of Job's integrity. Why this is never conveyed to Job remains an enigma.

We might ask: Had Job been told that the heavenly plot was the root of all his misery, would it have offered him any comfort? Rabbi Joshua Sperka, a contemporary writer, remarks: "There is a very comforting thought that can be drawn from the reading of this book. Here Job suffers not for punishment for sin, but as a test of his faith."[5] In fact, only the reader has access to this "very comforting thought." No one in the book ever mentions it to Job, who is so desperately in need of comfort, neither his friends, who are totally unaware of it, nor God, who prefers to conceal it. But is this thought indeed "very comforting" for the sufferer or even for the reader, as Sperka claims? Which kind of suffering is least objectionable — punitive, instructive, or explorative — is open to debate. It is doubtful whether Job would have found the explanation that his suffering is but a test of faith comforting — let alone morally defensible.

Ask yourself: Would you feel less hurt to be told that your troubles are because you are a good person and are being tested than to be told that you are a bad person and are being punished?

When bad things happen to people whom you wish to comfort,

would you feel that you need first to ascertain whether they are good people or bad people to determine how to console them? Our ingrained moral sensitivity dictates that a judgmental approach has no place within the delicate realm of consoling people who suffer. We must see them not as good or bad people, but rather as anguished people who need our help and sympathy, not our moralizing.

The Book of Job raises many complex issues, ranging from theological speculations to social ethics. It inspires difficult questions, but does not presume to provide facile answers. Some of these questions are answerable on a variety of levels and from different perspectives. Most of them, however, remain unanswerable. The Book of Job is replete with intriguing inconsistencies, paradoxical tensions, and subtle ironies, all of which are to be viewed not as flaws but rather as the exquisite features of a great masterpiece.

The Triangle of Trials and Interactions: Job, God, Friends

The Book of Job can be viewed as a triangle of trials and interactions among three main parties: *Job* (J), *God* (G), *Job's Friends* (F). Each of the three participants interacts with the other two, and each, explicitly or implicitly, is placed on trial.

Job, the book's hero, the suffering and protesting figure of the drama, is the innocent victim of divine testing and affliction. He is introduced in the prologue as a model of human righteousness and becomes the universal prototype of undeserved suffering and courageous protestation against divine injustice.

God, in the Jobian drama, is the Supreme Ruler of the universe, creator of the natural order and master over human destiny. He is on trial in Job's speeches.

Job's friends, who appear on the stage as comforters, soon start to defend God and accuse Job. By acting so, they displease both — arousing God's wrath (42:7) and aggravating Job's anguish.

The triangle of trials and interactions will be explored in detail in the next three chapters of this guide.

Discussion Questions:

1. Reflect on the active role of the reader in the dramatic experience which is accomplished by intimate interaction between reader and text. Show how the reader, by active, responsive, interpretive, and re-creative participation, brings the text to life.
2. A biblical parallel to the drama of Job is the *akedah* (binding of Isaac, Genesis 22). Both stories share the gripping theme of *nisayon*, divine testing of human faith. Compare these two cases.
3. Adele Berlin, *Poetics and the Interpretation of Biblical Narrative* (Sheffield: Almond Press, 1983), p. 54, points to the similarity in the beginnings of the *akedah* and *Job*:

The reader is given knowledge which the main characters do not have — in both these cases it is the knowledge that God is testing them. Obviously it would not be a valid test if Abraham and Job knew about it. The question is: Why is the reader told from the outset? The answer is that this allows him to perceive the events differently from the way that the characters do. For the characters, the question is: What does God want of me and why is he doing this to me? For the reader, the question is: Will Abraham/Job pass the test? Our knowledge that it is a test lets us accept actions on the part of God that are contrary to our picture of him. *Without* this knowledge we would be puzzled and/or incensed, much as Job is; *with* this knowledge we accept God's actions, knowing that He does not really intend them to be carried out.

Does Berlin's answer satisfy you? Does the reader's foreknowledge that the ordeal is just a test mitigate his/her outrage? Do we, the "knowing" readers of either of these two stories, the *akedah* or Job, really "accept actions on the part of God that are contrary" to our image of God? Would you distinguish between the two cases? As for the *akedah*, an argument can, perhaps, be made that we "accept" the actions, since we know "that He [God] does not really intend them to be carried out." Would you agree with this argument? Consider that Isaac, during the rest of his post-*akedah* life, remains a victim-survivor; that Sara, upon hearing of the *akedah*, dies (Midrash); and that Abraham after the *akedah* encounters God no more. As for Job's ordeal, how can one defend (or "accept") a divine intent that becomes a human tragedy?

Notes

1. Neither the title nor the cover page of Mitchell's work warn the reader, as they should, that this edition does *not* present the Book of Job in its entirety. In the last page are listed "Verses Deleted or Omitted" (which include, among many others, Elihu's speeches and Job's Hymn to Wisdom). This tampering with the book conjures up a different Job, not the biblical Job. Mitchell's edition can be used as a stimulating reference for comparison and discussion of the verses which are included, but not as a textbook for a study of Job in its entirety.

2. Students who wish to explore further the issue of the reader's role in interpretation and appreciation of biblical and literary texts will find the following sources helpful:

Edgar V. McKnight, *The Bible and the Reader: An Introduction to Literary Criticism* (Philadelphia: Fortress Press, 1985).

Wolfgang Iser, *The Act of Reading: A Theory of Aesthetic Response* (Baltimore: Johns Hopkins University Press, 1978).

Susan R. Suleiman and Inge Crosman (eds.), *The Reader in the Text: Essays on Audience and Interpretation* (Princeton University Press, 1980).

3. See chapter 1, "The Book of Job Within the Context of Biblical Literature," the paragraph on "The Three Wisdom Qualities as Reflected in the Book of Job," p. 8.

4. Babylonian Talmud, *Bava Batra*, 15b; see chapter 2, "The Hero," p. 15.

5. Joshua S. Sperka, *The Book of Job: Mankind on Trial* (New York: Bloch, 1979), p. 22.

◆ ◆ ◆

Chapter Five

Job On Trial

What Is The True Test Of Faith?

Required and Suggested Readings

Text (required):

Job 1:1-3:1; 42:6-17; 8:5-7; 8:20-22; 11:13-19; 22:21-28.

Supplementary Readings (suggested):

Horace M. Kallen, "Job the Humanist," in *Dimensions*, pp. 175-181.
Arthur S. Peake, "Job's Victory," in *Dimensions*, pp. 197-205.
Walter Kaufmann, "An Uncanny World," in *Dimensions*, pp. 237-245.
Soren Kierkegaard, "The Lord Gave, and the Lord Hath Taken
    Away," in *Dimensions*, pp. 253-268 (optional; difficult reading!).

Two On Trial In the Book of Job: Humanity and God

The Book of Job presents two parallel questions, one on human piety and the other on divine justice. In the first question, humankind is on trial; in the second, God is on trial. Both questions interrelate in the book's plots and speeches — the first dominates the prologue and the friends' speeches; the second is the overriding theme in Job's responses and soliloquies.

The first question is openly raised in the prologue (1:8-11; 2:2-5). In anthropomorphic imagery, God "boasts" before the *satan* that Job, His devotee, is a paradigm of piety. Challenging God's claim, the *satan* argues that Job's piety is not genuine but self-serving. Job is then put to the test — first in the prologue, through two phases of horrible torments, and then in the dialogues, through three cycles of his friends' speeches.

The Testing of Job

In the prologue, Job clearly passes both phases of his test. Mercilessly crushed, Job maintains his integrity; facing adversity, he keeps his faith. He does not blaspheme; he "accepts the bad from God," as he did before "accept the good." Thus Job proves that his piety is genuine.

Job's integrity is maintained throughout the entire book, even when he accuses God, demanding justice rather than pleading for mercy.

Job is also on trial in his friends' speeches, being judged from a different point of view. The friends' concept of piety is diametrically opposed to the one implied in the prologue. For them, piety and prosperity go hand in hand. If you are pious, you will prosper; if you are not, you will perish. If you suffer, this in itself indicates that you are lacking in piety. You must repent, pray for forgiveness, and become pious; then you will prosper again (8:5-7; 8:20-22; 11:13-19; 22:21-28).

Parallel to the physical and mental torment of Job in the prologue, the friends launch a massive assault, no less ferocious. They verbally abuse him and caustically attack his integrity — the drama's pivotal issue. Still, Job does not break. Up to his final verses he stands upright, confronting God and his friends. And, as the disputation continues, he grows even stronger.

Both Job and God emerge as the winners. Job passed the test, and God won the wager. This is implicit throughout the book's plots and dialogues, with no need by the author to press the point. Any sensitive reader will realize that Job passed the test of pure piety, not only by omission, that he did not blaspheme God, but also by commission, that he argued with God.

Job continued to wrestle with God, while at the same time he firmly clung to Him and maintained his integrity before Him. Thus Job proved that his piety was genuine, expressing love and devotion, not fear of punishment or anticipation of reward.

Consequently, Job will dare tell God what is on his mind because of — not despite — his true devotion to God! Ironically, Job passed his test of genuine piety by forcefully, yet honestly, accusing God. And God won the wager by becoming the target for Job's accusations.

The core of the test is not whether Job can control his rage — "Will he curb or unleash his urge to curse God?" — but whether Job's devotion to God is firmly unconditional. The authenticity of Job's faith — not his patience[1] — is at stake: "Will he, even in adversity, continue to cling to God, or will he then renounce Him altogether?" This is essentially what "cursing" God means: expressing contempt and rejection, "I have no use for You!"

Both Job's wife and his friends fail. The wife, who figures as the instigator — for it is she (not the *satan*) who incites Job! — is ineffective in inducing Job to curse God. The friends, defenders of traditional theology, are unsuccessful in convincing Job to submit to God. Job remains steadfast. Rebuffing his wife, he does not renounce God; defying his friends, he does not flatter Him.

Had Job listened to either voice — that of his wife to curse God, or of his friends to submit to Him — he would have failed the test. Job would have then proven that his piety, as the *satan* claimed, reflected his pursuit of material success rather than true religious devotion. Truthful to the core, Job neither surrendered to God nor blasphemed Him.

What is the Difference Between Blasphemy and Protestation?

When Job accuses God of injustice, he comes close to blasphemy. How is reproaching God a less severe offense than cursing Him? Is protesting God not a form of blasphemy?

The two are not the same. Blasphemy is renouncing God; protestation is the reverse, demanding and expecting justice from God.

Cursing God is a desperate act of one who lost his faith; arguing with Him is the courageous stance of one who clings to his faith. Only a genuinely pious person can be moved to rail against God as Job does.

This is the essence of Job's dilemma. The fire of his grievances against God, kindled by his personal misery, is inflamed by the passion of his faith. It is because of his faith in God that Job cannot tolerate injustice on the part of God. Job judges God by the ideal of justice which is ingrained in his heart by virtue of his faith in God. Despite all that has happened to him, Job refuses to "curse God and die" (wife's view) or to flatter God and live (friends' view), because he steadfastly remains God's devotee (God's view). Even in his anger and frustration, Job continues to maintain his love of God.

Job rejects his friends' counsel that he confess and surrender to God. Why? Precisely because he loves Him, he tenaciously maintains his integrity before Him. Job does not accept his friends' arguments in defense of God. Why? Because, as he sees it, the friends are trying to defend wrong as right, injustice as justice! They are devaluing Job's idea of God. Job cannot accept a defense of God which insults the dignity of God. Thus Job has passed his test and God has won the wager!

Two Contrasting Views on Human Piety and Suffering

Ironically, both Job's friends and the *satan* share the same somber, pragmatic view on the nature of human piety. The friends, unaware of the heavenly scenes in the prologue, are remarkably in agreement with the view of the *satan*, that there is no piety for its own sake. This dismal outlook is contrary to the expressed view of God, Who expects from Job — and trusts that Job will show Him — genuine, selfless devotion.

The friends — in accord with the *satan*, and not with God — express their conviction that piety is by its very nature self-serving. But, in dissension with both the *satan* and God, they seem to see nothing wrong with this kind of piety.

What an irony! Job is on trial to prove that his piety is independent of reward. He is then placed on trial again by his friends for precisely the opposite charge: his stubborn refusal to embrace self-serving piety, which is deemed worthless in the heavenly court.

The contrast between the two views of human integrity — the prologue's and the friends' — is staggering. The view in Heaven is that a person's religious and moral conduct (even if perfect) when motivated by expectation of material gain, does not merit any credit.

The friends maintain the opposite view: A person's piety is rooted in the quest for success and gratification — one's "pursuit of happiness." Devotion to God is thus nourished by the conviction that God rewards loyalty.

This very point determines the striking contrast between the prologue and the dialogues concerning the meaning of human suffering. The friends in the dialogues accuse Job while zealously defending God. Paradoxically, they agree with the *satan*'s position in the prologue that Job's piety is motivated by his success and will be shaken by his troubles (1:10-11; 4:5-6), but they disagree with the heavenly court on the meaning of Job's suffering. Job's ordeal, ordained in Heaven as a test, is perceived by his friends as a punishment. His anguish, projected in the prologue as a result of his piety, is taken by his friends as a proof of his impiety.

In the epilogue it becomes clear that the friends were wrong all along in their judgment. The friends are rebuked, Job is rewarded, and his fortunes restored.

This happy ending leaves the reader bewildered. Is this the divine reward for Job's steadfastness throughout his ordeal or for his final moment of precipitous surrender? Did Job earn his bliss because of his relentless, fierce protestation against God, as displayed throughout the dialogues, or because of his alleged submission before God, as reflected in his final response to God's revelation "out of the whirlwind" (42:6)?

The Vindication of Job: Did Job Finally Repent and Surrender?

We must pay attention to the literary design of the book. The epilogue makes no reference at all to this revelational encounter between Job and God or to Job's "change of heart." Nor is it clear from Job's response (42:6) what exactly he does "regret" — his assertive arguments with God or his misery, despair, self-pity? Did Job at last "submit" to God, as was demanded all along by his friends?

A careful reading of Job's final words may lead the reader to the opinion that Job never really surrendered. Job has not confessed to any offenses (which he has never committed), nor has he ever yielded to his friends' speeches or followed their advice (which he has consistently rejected). Resisting his friends' preachings, rather than complying with them, Job, at the end of the dialogues, experiences self-recovery, self-realization, and gains a renewed self-esteem.[2]

Students who perceive Job's final words to be an admission of guilt, and the happy conclusion as a reward for the hero's "remorse" and a divine forgiveness for his previous "stubbornness,"[3] are missing the whole point of the book. Job — not the friends, not even God! — has been vindicated. Job has insisted on his innocence to the last moment; he has never yielded to his friends and has never confessed to God. He has maintained his integrity to the end (27:6).

If we say that Job did finally repent, one might wonder what took him so long? Why did Job not give in at the beginning of the story? What is the point of holding out for so long, until, finally, he acknowledges his guilt and confesses the impropriety of arguing with God? The underlying message of the book, however, is that Job's arguments with God — combative and poignant as they sound — are heroic and praiseworthy (42:7)!

Job was explicitly put to the test by God, and he passed; the friends were implicitly tested by Job's condition, and they failed. Job passed the test of piety; the friends failed the test of friendship.

This point is evident to the careful reader of the Book of Job, who must wonder: Why is Job rewarded by God at the end of the story, while his friends, who have tried to bring Job close to God, are spurned by God? But, did the friends indeed want "to bring Job to God" or rather to bring him "on his knees" before God? Did they envision reconciliation or surrender?

Job would not surrender. At the end, he recovered. And by virtue of his integrity he was able to bring about a reconciliation between himself and God. Therefore, while his friends were spurned by God, Job was greatly rewarded.

Discussion Questions:

1. Consider the various views projected in the book on the correlation between Job's piety and prosperity. Restate, in your own terms, the views of God, the *satan*, the friends — as applied to yourself or to people you know. What is your own view on this issue? How do you perceive a correlation, if at all, between moral or religious conduct and success in life?

2. Let us assume that Job fails his prologue test — he acts as the *satan* anticipates and his wife suggests; he blasphemes God — do you fault him? Does Job, by your standards, fail or pass the test? Explain.

3. When a person's good conduct, moral or religious, is motivated by expectation of reward, material or spiritual, or by fear of punishment — is this conduct, in your opinion, blameless, flawed, or worthless?

4. Based on your own experience or judgment, how does individual integrity, moral or religious, affect potential for, and attitude toward, material gain? And, the reverse: how does personal success affect potential for, and attitude toward, moral or religious perfection?

5. In your view, is it right or wrong to expect reward, either from God or from society, for moral or religious good conduct? Does anticipation of reward diminish the value of good deeds?

6. How can a modern person, living in a success-oriented society with its feverish pursuit of individual happiness, relate to the Jobian concept of selfless devotion to God?

Notes

1. The proverbial "Job's patience" is a contributing factor in the common misunderstanding of Job. The idiom derives from Christian preachings rooted in the New Testament (James 5:11), praising the virtue of patience by pointing to Job as its biblical model. In the popular mind, Job has thus become a model of pious submission to God, a man who patiently and serenely suffered God's "arrows" of outrageous abuse without complaining. But Job did complain, and did protest, emerging indeed, as perceived in the Jewish tradition, as the protestor *par excellence*. Job's alleged "patience" is probably based on semantic inaccuracy, the term originally referring not to his indifference or forbearance, but rather to his endurance and steadfastness — Job's firmness, not resignation, before God.

2. See chapter 8, "Job's Recovery," p. 71 and "Job's Recovery Chart," p. 80.

3. This view is commonly held by commentators.

◆ ◆ ◆

Chapter Six

God On Trial

"Will The Judge Of All The Universe Not Do Justice?!"

Required and Suggested Readings

Text (required):

Job 9:22-24; 11:13-15; 30:19; 42:6.
Genesis 18:17-33; Isaiah 1:15; Jeremiah 12:1-2; Habakkuk 1:13.

Supplementary Readings (suggested):

Eliezer Berkovits, "God and the Holocaust," in *Faith After the Holocaust* (New York: Ktav, 1973), pp. 67-85.
Martin Buber, "A God Who Hides His Face," in *Dimensions*, pp. 56-65.
Harold Kushner, "The Story of a Man Named Job," in *When Bad Things Happen to Good People* (New York: Schocken, 1981), pp. 31-46.
Robert Gordis, *The Book of Job: Commentary, New Translation and Special Studies* (New York: Jewish Theological Seminary, 1978), p. 108.
Joshua S. Sperka, *The Book of Job: Mankind on Trial* (New York: Bloch, 1979), Introduction.

KRAVITZ MEMORIAL LIBRARY
of Park Synagogue

90 -241

God is Challenged by the Prophets

Accusing God is sanctioned in the Jewish prophetic tradition. Abraham, Jeremiah, and Habakkuk, each in his own way challenges God with courage and vigor.[1] Jeremiah decries the success of evildoers:

> Righteous You are, O Lord,
> That I would dare dispute with You!
> Yet, I must contend with You!
> Why is the way of the wicked prosperous?
> [Why do] the treacherous live in contentment?[2]

Jeremiah introduces his complaint reverently, affirming that God *is* righteous! Yet, precisely because of God's righteousness, the prophet must "contend with" Him or "talk *mishpatim*" — speak reproachfully — to God.

Jeremiah's grievance is the prosperity of the wicked, rather than the misery of the innocent. His explicit question is, "Why is the way of the wicked prosperous?" Not, "Why is the way of the innocent perilous?" In effect he asks, "Why are good things happening to bad people?" Not, "Why are bad things happening to good people?"

The prophet's question echoes not so much our distress about the misfortunes of deserving persons, but rather the broader concern about the success of the oppressors. The modern question is focused on the individual's welfare, which is presumed to be his entitlement from God. The prophetic question reflects a universal vision of social justice, which is demanded of both God and humanity.

The two questions are related. The success of the wicked is a result and a cause of their oppression of the innocent. When the oppressors prosper, the vicious cycle of tyranny and misery is set into motion. Jeremiah's quintessential question is: Why does the power of the mighty prevail over the needs of the weak?

Habakkuk goes even further. Caustically he asks God:

Are your eyes too pure to look at evil;
Is the sight of misery too much for You to bear?!
Why, then, do you [passively] gaze at the treacherous;
[Why] do You remain silent,
when the wicked one (*rasha*)
devours the one who is more righteous than he?![3]

Habakkuk uses satire to deplore God's indifference to the rule of "the wicked one" (*rasha*): Why are You silent? Are Your eyes too pure to look at evil? Is it beneath You to look at human misery? Are You too sensitive to confront evil and suffering? Is that why You simply ignore them?

Job follows the argumentative line of Hebrew prophecy. There is reason to put God on trial. Where is divine providence? Where is divine benevolence? Where is divine justice? The reality of human suffering negates the theory of divine justice. This is Job's stance.

The Friends React

Now, Job's friends are outraged. In order to resolve Job's dilemma, they are bent on seeing in Job's suffering a manifestation of God's justice. By doing so, they demonstrate the harshness of simplistic dogma. They "comfort" Job by urging him to turn to God and remove evil from himself (11:13-15):

If you direct your heart [toward God],
and stretch out the palms of your hands toward Him —
If iniquity be in your hands, remove it;
let not injustice reside in your tent —
Surely then you may lift up your face, free of blemish;
You may stand firm, unafraid!

The friends' response is replete with the poetic imagery of body language in prayer. This imagery involves the worshipper's heart, palms of his hands, and face: first, his heart, the inward preparation for appealing to God; then, the palms of his hands, spreading them openly toward God, in an outward gesture of supplication; and finally, his face, looking upward in expectation of God's favor.

This poetic portrayal of prayer by Zophar, which starts with a promising "*if*" — "If you set your heart . . ." — deceptively appears as comforting. But then comes another, scolding and demanding "*if*" — "If iniquity be in your hands. . . ." Zophar's imagery is prophetically inspired. *If* the worshipper stretches out his hands to God, he is then taking a chance, for *if* his hands are not clean — if they are tainted with blood or illegal possessions — the dishonest worshipper puts himself in jeopardy. God will remove His eyes from the worshipper and his prayers will not be heard.[4]

The friendly suggestion that Job remove "iniquity" (*aven*) from his hand and not allow "injustice" (*avla*) to dwell within his tent implies more than shunning evil conduct. It conveys a literal demand upon Job: restitution of stolen property, wealth gained by deception or exploitation, to its rightful owners.[5]

In line with the Jewish sense of justice, the friends imply that Job must first remove from his "hands" all the stolen goods and restore them to their rightful owners. Then, and only then, will he be entitled to God's pardon.[6] The friends would rather blame Job than God, place a man on trial but not God.

God's verdict (42:7), which takes the reader by surprise, delivers the book's message clearly and succinctly. To put God on trial is not an act of defiance but of faith. It is the right and duty of the person who cares for justice, and expects and demands justice from God.

This is the core idea of the Book of Job: that God may be challenged by a genuinely pious person, and the person by doing so does not forfeit, but rather fortifies, his or her faith. This is the example of Job, who remonstrated with God out of his own sufferings. This is also the example of Abraham, who protested out of his concern for the sufferings of others.[7]

Our Right and Duty to Claim Justice From God: Job and Abraham As Examples

The idea that a human being has the right and duty to demand divine justice is demonstrated by two great biblical heroes, Job and Abraham: Job, the universal prototype of righteousness and suffering, and Abraham, the first patriarch of the Jewish people. Each epitomizes the human quest for divine justice. Job defiantly maintains his moral integrity. Abraham, wrestling with God over the fate of Sodom and Gomorrah, demands that God act justly: "Will the Judge of all the universe not do justice?!"[8]

Each case is unique. Job is a tormented individual; Abraham, a concerned patriarch. Job wrestles with God out of his own personal agony; Abraham, out of his concern for the agony of other people. Job is struggling to be relieved from his private pain and be vindicated; Abraham, to save others from doom. In contrast to Job's case, where God is silent on the issue of justice,[9] in Abraham's case, God initially inspires the hero to assess all conduct, divine as well as human, by the cosmic ideal of "*tzedakah u-mishpat*" — righteousness and justice. This binary phrase expresses a single idea, "true justice," which is to become the hallmark of historic Judaism.[10]

The whole encounter between Abraham and God was initiated by God: "Shall I hide from Abraham what I am going to do? Abraham, after all, is destined to become a great and mighty nation ... for I have favored him, because (or, in order that) he will instruct his children and his family to keep the way of God, to do *tzedakah u-mishpat....*"[11]

Abraham — in his demand for universal justice, his concern for the tragic fate of others — exquisitely demonstrates the Torah's doctrine of involvement, conveyed by a classic verse in Leviticus: "Do not stand still (doing nothing), while your fellow is bleeding!"[12] Namely, when your fellow's life is at stake, rush to his side and rescue him. Be not indifferent when the life of another human being is in jeopardy.

This verse, underlying Abraham's "involvement" and moral outrage, has served as a model for Judaism.[13] This pristine Jewish doctrine — the moral and legal duty of involvement in order to save others — is nobly represented by Abraham. In the Jewish spirit of involvement, Abraham intervenes with God on behalf of the condemned cities.

Job, on the other hand, serves as a universal representative of the noble individual who is outraged by his own suffering. But, after facing his own misery, Job, too, develops a passionate concern for the misery of others. In line with Abraham, he rails against all forms of injustice, on both levels, personal as well as societal — as illustrated in Job's "Wicked One" passage.

Job Indicts God: The "Wicked One"

Job — who through his ordeal maintains his integrity — places God on trial. The following accusatory passage astonishes us with its boldness (9:22-24):

> It is all one!
> Therefore I say:
> Whether innocent or guilty, He destroys him.
> When a whip suddenly kills,
> It mocks the anguish of the pure ones.
> The earth is placed in the hand of a wicked one;
> He covers the faces of its judges!
> If not so, then who is He?

"It is all one" (*ahat he!*). Thus begins the opening verse (9:22), which, according to Robert Gordis, "is probably the strongest indictment of God to be found in the book."[14] The Hebraic phrase, idiomatic for "it is all the same," is an exclamation of indifference: "Nothing matters!" This has a double implication, referring to both Job and God (the speaker and his subject matter): It makes no difference — either to me, or to Him.

To Job: It makes no difference to me; therefore I am not afraid to speak up. Whether I rail against God or submit to Him, my fate is sealed, it will remain the same: "Therefore I [dare] say...."

To God: It makes no difference to Him; therefore the world is in disarray. Whether one is destroyed or not, whether one is righteous or not, God does not care! As if the world is ruled not by moral design, but by caprice and randomness.

The lack of moral discrimination in the conduct of the world is illustrated by the imagery of the deadly whip (*shot*): "It mocks the anguish of the pure ones" — "it" referring to the personified, scourging whip (*shot*). When it is unleashed to suddenly kill, it "mocks" at the victims' pleas. We expect no compassion from an inanimate tool, a whip, which can have no regard for human anguish. Ironically, this whip is not merely inanimate. It takes on human depravity; it is cruel. Certainly the one who unleashes the whip is cruel. The Hebrew for "it mocks" may also be rendered as "he mocks" or "He mocks" — referring to the ruler (human or divine) who is responsible for unleashing the scourging whip, which may represent both natural and man-made disasters.

Who is "the wicked one" (*rasha*) in Job's imagery? In whose hand is the earth placed? A human despot or God?

Job's words are uttered in the twilight, within the border of two domains, the terrestrial and the celestial, reverberating in both. On the external level of meaning, Job refers to a human tyrant (local or global). In a deeper, internal sense, Job points to Heaven. As dramatized in the prologue, Earth is ruled by Heaven.

According to a bold rabbinic view, Job points to God Himself, implying that He is the "Wicked One"![15] Another view modifies this interpretation: Job refers not directly to God, but to His *satan*. This interpretation is unlikely; Job, after all, is unaware of the *satan's* role. Besides, this makes Job only slightly less confrontational. The *satan* does not operate independently, nor is he God's antagonist. He is God's appointed employee. God alone is responsible.

Job concludes (9:24): "If not so, then who is He?" This rhetorical question is both subtle and poignant. It entails a double connotation: "Who is He?" (referring to God), and "Who is he?" (referring to a human being). Referring to God ("He") is more in keeping with the Jobian mood of placing God on trial: If what I describe, concerning the rampant injustice in the world, is true, then who is God? What kind of a God is He? Where is He? Why does He not maintain justice on earth? The verse is at the same time a rhetorical challenge to his friends to dare repudiate his drastic statement: If what I say is not true, then who is the person ("he") who will prove me wrong? (Compare 24:25.)

Job vigorously demands justice from God. The student is compelled to ask: Is it proper to speak this way to God? What does God's reaction imply? What do I personally think? Conceivably, many students of the book would prefer a more reverent Job. Joshua Sperka's work on the book bears the telling title, *The Book of Job: Mankind on Trial*; the author remarks:

> I am incensed at the flippancy of many writers on the Book of Job whose interpretations put G-d on trial. That is the reason for the title of this book: *Job — Mankind on Trial*.[16]

No doubt that mankind is put on trial in the Book of Job, but so is God.

Dust and Ashes

This Hebrew biblical concept of placing "God on trial" is balanced by the pervasive awareness of God's supremacy. Remarkably, both Abraham and Job use the same metaphor "dust and ashes."[17] This phrase describes the hero's humanness and mortality, even as he challenges God. Abraham uses this phrase apologetically: "See, I beg, how I dare to speak to My Lord, [*though*] I am but dust and ashes!"[18] Job, echoing Abraham, uses this phrase twice. In his soliloquy, he reflects (30:19): "He (God) has thrown me into the mud, so that I see myself as dust and ashes."[19] In his final line to God (42:6), commonly perceived as an expression of remorse and surrender, he muses: "…wherefore I abhor *myself*, and repent in dust and ashes."[20]

This popular rendition of Job's final line[21] — "in dust and ashes" as a gesture of self-humiliation — interprets the Hebrew verb *nahem* as "repent" (regret or relent), expressing Job's contrition and submission. This is untenable. Since Job is innocent, of what sins does he now repent?

We must reconsider the translation of the Hebrew verb used by Job, *nahem*. It connotes an additional meaning of comfort and consolation (as in the Hebrew noun *nehamah*[22]). Job's final verse thus says: "Therefore I abhor [*my misery*], and will seek and find comfort, [*though*] I am wallowing in dust and ashes."

Both Abraham and Job are aware of their mortality. Abraham compares himself to "dust and ashes" and Job wallows in them.[23] Yet, both demonstrate their power to transcend their human fragility and, standing tall before God, they dare to contend with Him, question Him, demand justice from Him, and accuse Him of not administering His universe justly.

Overwhelmed by God's voice from the whirlwind, Job seeks to be consoled for being mere dust and ashes. Fully recovered, Job regrets his existential worthlessness, but not his imaginary transgressions nor his relentless demand for justice from God.

Job was placed on trial by God, and at last he was vindicated. God was placed on trial by Job. Was He vindicated?

Discussion Questions:

1. Consider the value of "involvement" in Judaism (Leviticus 19:16). As suggested above, this precept is illustrated by Abraham's drive to protect the innocent, by protesting before God in demand of justice. How is this example related to modern society? Think of different ways of involvement, to protect and save lives. Relate this concept to Hadassah.

2. Imagine a moral system devoid of the duty of "involvement" and relate it to our modern world — the present situation of Israel and the past horror of the Holocaust.

3. Check and examine different English translations to Leviticus 19:16, and react to them.

4. Compare the prophetic outrage against injustice, divine or human, with our modern outrage: "When bad things happen to good people" (Kushner). Discuss the problem and its suggested solutions. Show how both types of moral outrage, the prophetic and the modern, inspire our ways of coping with adversity.

5. Do you consider divine justice to be a gift from God or a human right that we can demand from Him? What do we learn from Abraham and Job? How does our approach to divine justice affect our insistence upon human justice?

6. Consider God's final verdict (42:7), rebuking the friends and vindicating Job. What does it suggest about the authenticity of the idea of placing God on trial?

7. Reflect on the "dust and ashes" phrase uttered by Abraham (Genesis 18:26) and Job (42:6). Consider what is common in both cases and what is unique in each one. How do you relate to this human awareness of being in "dust and ashes" and what does it mean to you?

8. Read Anne Roiphe's *A Season for Healing* (New York: Summit Books, 1987). What is her basic thesis? Do you agree with it in light of your reading on Job and on the Holocaust?

Notes

1. Genesis 18:25; Jeremiah 12:1; Habakkuk 1:13.
2. Jeremiah 12:1.
3. Habakkuk 1:13.
4. Compare Isaiah 1:15.
5. The Hebrew terms for "iniquity" and "injustice" (*aven* and *avla*) indicate more than abstractions; they refer to concrete objects obtained by fraudulence and deceit. Babylonian Talmud, *Ketubot* 19a-b.
6. See Leviticus 5:23; compare Isaiah 3:14; Ezekiel 18:13; 33:15.
7. Genesis 18:25.
8. *Ibid.*

9. Note that nowhere in the Book of Job, including His final revelation to Job, does God assert His attribute of justice.

10. The two nouns are taken as one, which is known as *hendiadys*.

11. Genesis 18:17-19.

12. Leviticus 19:16. "Do not stand..." (*lo ta'amod*) parallels "Do not go..." (*lo telekh*) of the first half of the verse. Both couplets of the verse are poetically connected. In the private affairs of others, do not get involved ("don't go!"), don't gossip; but, when others are bleeding, become involved ("don't stand!"), you must actively save their lives!

13. This Hebraic doctrine is not conveyed in English by any of the current Christian translations of this biblical verse. One single, laudable exception is the 1970 *New American Bible* (Catholic), which, inspired by the "Old" JPS (Jewish Publication Society translation of 1917), renders the verse properly: "...nor shall you stand by idly when your neighbor's life is at stake." It is to the credit of the first Jewish translation of Hebrew Scriptures in America ("Old" JPS) that the correct meaning of this crucial verse has been introduced. Regrettably, the rendering in the "New" JPS is a terrible blunder and must be discarded.

14. Robert Gordis, *The Book of Job: Commentary, New Translation and Special Studies* (New York: Jewish Theological Seminary, 1978), p. 108.

15. Rabbi Eliezer, Babylonian Talmud, *Bava Batra*, 16a.

16. Joshua Sperka, *The Book of Job: Mankind on Trial* (New York: Bloch, 1979), Introduction.

17. Abraham in Genesis 18:27; Job, in his soliloquy, 30:19, and in his response to God's final revelation, 42:6. Remarkably, no other person, in all Hebrew Scriptures, uses this phrase.

18. Genesis 18:27.

19. The Hebrew verb "*va-etmashel*" (from the trilateral root *m-sh-l*, in the reflexive) conveys a double meaning of likeness and parable (which commonly uses metaphor or simile). The verb thus connotes ideas of both being compared to and being a proverb: "I have become in my eyes as the proverbial 'dust and ashes.'"

20. This is the rendition of the "authorized" King James Version (1611). The italics in the phrase "I abhor *myself*" indicate that "myself" is not found in the original Hebrew text; it is the translator's addition. The Jewish rendition (in the Old JPS of 1917), probably uncomfortable with the excessive meekness in the KJV rendition, replaced "myself" with "my words" — substituting unwarranted remorse for unconscionable self-denigration — and left intact the ending "and repent in dust and ashes." The "New" JPS rendition is essentially the old idea in a different garb: "Therefore, I recant and relent / Being but dust and ashes."

21. The KJV rendition ("repent") is generally adopted — with slight variations ("regret," "relent," or "recant") — by all current biblical translations.

22. Rashi.

23. Job's ultimate situation "in dust and ashes" corresponds in part to his initial one: In pain, Job "sits within the ashes" (2:8).

◆ ◆ ◆

Chapter Seven

Job's Friends On Trial
Theology Versus Friendship

Required and Suggested Readings

Text (required):

Job 2:11-3:1; 4:1-11:20; 34:1-37:24; 42:7-17.
Leviticus 25:17; Psalms 37 and 73.

Supplementary Readings (suggested):

David Wolfers, "Elihu: The Provenance and Content of His
    Speeches," *Dor le Dor, Our Biblical Heritage*, volume 16, number 2
    (winter 1987/88), pp. 90-98.
Hans Ehrenberg, "Elihu the Theologian," in *Dimensions*, pp. 93-100.
Lewis S. Feuer, "The Book of Job: The Wisdom of Hebraic Stoicism,"
    in *Biblical vs. Secular Ethics: The Conflict*, edited by R. Joseph
    Hoffman and Gerald A. Larue (Buffalo, New York: Prometheus
    Books, 1988), pp. 79-97.
Maurice Lamm, *The Jewish Way in Death and Mourning* (New York:
    Ktav, 1969).

Between the Friends and Job

Job's three friends arrive together, each from his own place, to be with Job, "to show sympathy to him and comfort him" (2:11-12). With ceremonial decorum, "they lifted up their eyes from afar" to gaze at Job, "but could not recognize him." Job's readers, together with Job's friends, now become shockingly aware of Job's disfigured appearance. The astounded friends "lifted up their voices and broke into loud weeping." The verb "lifted up" is effectively repeated, first for the "eyes" and then for the "voices," the agents of human impression and expression.

The friends then perform the customary rituals of mourning. They rend their clothes, throw dust upon their heads, and gesture "toward Heaven." Thus, in body language, the friends point to God as the sole source of Job's misfortune, as well as his only hope.

The "triangle" of interactions among the three parties — God, Job, and the friends — is now symbolically drawn. Looking up to Heaven (to God), sitting down on the ground (with Job), the friends close the dramatic triangle.

The friends start their condolence visit politely, in utter silence (2:13):

> They sat down on the ground with him,
> for seven days and seven nights.
> And none of them spoke a word to him;
> for they saw how very great was the pain.

This is in accord with Jewish custom.[1] The consolers remain silent and wait for the mourner to initiate conversation. As long as the mourner does not speak, the consolers share in the silence. They are there with the mourner to offer their comforting presence and warm closeness, to offer help and relief, to listen; not to intrude, not to encumber the mourner with words. Words, more often than not, are a burden. No wonder that both speech and burden are called in Hebrew, *masa*.

Out of respect to Job, the friends curb their urge to speak; they see this effort as heroic.[2] As a courtesy they carry the burden of silence for a full week (as long as Job remains silent), "for they saw how very great was the pain."

The Hebrew style is precise: "the pain," not "his pain."[3] This reflects the friends' acute awareness of "the pain" in general, not just Job's personal pain, but the pain universally shared by all who are present in Job's company. They defer to this pain in silence.

Job initiates the dialogue. He begins the discussion with an outburst of curses. He curses neither God nor friends, but the day of his birth — condemning his own existence, rejecting the very gift of life, and expressing suicidal wishes. The narrative is very specific (3:1). After seven days and seven nights of eloquent silence: "Job opened his mouth, and cursed his day...." Job's "opening of his mouth" to speak is reported as a significant event. It marks the dialogue's official starting point.

From now on the friends feel entitled, perhaps even obligated, to speak. Now they will respond, not intrude. There is a touch of gentleness in the first verse of the friends' speeches, as Eliphaz conveys his formal request for permission from Job to speak to him (4:1):

> Should one attempt to speak to you,
> would you get tired?
> For who can manage
> to hold back his words?

Yet, these polite words are uttered with affectation, not with affection. The opening verse is formal and transparent. Once the friends begin speaking, they mince no words and reveal themselves as harsh and cold.

Throughout all their lengthy speeches, the three friends never call Job by name. They refer to him directly or indirectly with anonymous pronouns (*you* or *he*), but never call him Job. Job responds in kind; he never mentions their names either. Does this style convey a sense of chilling remoteness and alienation, or is it, perhaps, a gesture of respectful distance? It certainly illustrates a lack of warmth and closeness.

This point is subtly indicated by a narrative detail which tells how the friends appear on the scene (2:12). They look at Job "from afar" (*merahok*) and "could not recognize him" (*velo hikiruhu*). From the start to the end of the drama, the friends relate to Job in the same way; they remain both distant and estranged.

The Fourth Speaker — Elihu

Remarkably, the fourth, the late-comer, young Elihu, who seems to enjoy no personal relationship with Job and is never referred to in the book as Job's friend — in contrast to the three "official" friends — does repeatedly refer to Job by name. Talking to Job (33:1): "But now, Job, listen to my words." Turning to the general audience (34:7): "What man is like Job, who drinks mockery like water?" And rebuking the friends (32:12): "I followed you attentively, and behold, none of you qualifies as *mokhiah* — 'debater' or preacher (one who can prove his point) — against Job!" Elihu the non-conformist demonstrates that, unlike the friends, he addresses Job by name. The author presents Elihu as a foil for the others.

Thus the reader is made aware of the glaring absence of Job's name in the speeches of the three friends who precede Elihu. The reader is left to wonder why, and to explore the meaning of addressing someone by name in the etiquette of Job's society. Is it a show of respect or excessive familiarity? Are the three friends overly aloof, or is young Elihu boldly arrogant?

Elihu Compared with Job's Three Friends

Elihu's speeches are distinguished from those of the three friends in both content and style. His orations are sparklingly refreshing, his demeanor more assertive, his expressions highly impassioned. He is bold yet warm, verbose but provocative. Ironically, Elihu comes too late, and his stormy orations elicit no reaction whatever from Job or from his friends. Elihu is completely ignored in the book's narrative, even by God. In the epilogue, the three friends are recognized — God says to Eliphaz (42:9): "I am angry at you and your two friends..." — but He does not mention Elihu. God's reference to Bildad and Zophar as the "two friends" of Eliphaz, rather than to all of them as the friends of Job, is indicative. It makes the reader wonder whether God does indeed view them as Job's friends.

Job too is mentioned in God's final words to Eliphaz, but emphatically, not as "your friend," instead as "My devotee" *(avdi)*. And Elihu? He is neither recognized nor considered. His appearance is clamorous, his departure quiet.

Unlike Elihu, the three friends left their impact on Job, but it was the reverse of their intent. Aiming to break him, they fortified his resistance; intent upon humbling him, they restored his self-esteem. Presuming to console him, they became aggressive accusers; the would-be defenders turned out to be relentless prosecutors.

Job's friends act under the pious pretext of guarding both God's honor and Job's welfare. Religion, which they offer to Job as a remedy, becomes their weapon. Their religious preaching turns to verbal abuse. To appreciate the irony of beneficent yet cruel counseling, let us examine how Job's friends lecture him on the doctrine of divine retribution.

Preaching Divine Retribution: Is It Consolation?

Eliphaz, in his very first speech, preaches divine retribution. He proclaims that the dogma of divine reward and punishment does operate in this world — all evidence to the contrary notwithstanding! He confronts Job with the following rhetorical questions (4:7):

> Remember, please:
> What innocent person has ever been destroyed?
> Where have the upright been annihilated?!

While Eliphaz seems to expect of his audience a pious denial — "*None!*" "*Nowhere!*" — Job, and the readers with him, know in their hearts otherwise — "*Many* innocents are destroyed! *Everywhere* are the upright annihilated!" Is Eliphaz naive or insensitive?

Eliphaz's rhetoric is sanctimonious and unfounded. It is repudiated by human experience, past and present. Furthermore, it is negated by the prologue's representation of Job as "innocent" and "upright," and of his calamity as the result of his exceptional flawlessness. But this information has been given only to us, Job's readers, not to Job's friends. Do the friends really believe that Job is culpable?

The friends merely represent conventional theology. They echo the view articulated by the psalmist:

> Young I was and I have aged;
> yet I have never seen
> a righteous person forsaken;
> nor his descendants begging bread![4]

The faithful psalmist declares that he has never seen, throughout his long life, what we are all painfully witnessing throughout history: that the righteous are too often forsaken, and their children left hungry.

The psalmist ignores reality. Undoubtedly he has encountered "a righteous person forsaken," yet he sees only what he wants to see. The psalmist's verse is oblivious to both the agonies and the virtues of others. The Talmud insists that neither God nor human could have uttered such an absurd verse.[5]

Job's friends do not directly quote Scriptures or rely on the psalmist. Eliphaz invokes his own logic (4:17): "Can a mortal be more just than God? Can a person be more pure than his Maker?" Bildad relies on tautological reasoning (8:3): "Will God distort justice? Will the Almighty pervert righteousness?" Zophar dwells on humankind's inability to penetrate God's mystery (11:7): "Can you discover God's designs? Can you find God's purpose?"

In theory Job agrees with all these arguments. But, theory is one thing, reality is another. The friends' judgment of Job is prejudiced by their dogma of divine retribution; Job's struggle against their dogma is reinforced by his own experience. The friends concur with Psalm 37. They too, incredible as it seems, "have never seen an innocent person destroyed or the upright annihilated." Now, they expect Job to ignore his shocking reality and embrace their pious theory.

Eliphaz's reply to Job blends facile encouragement with harsh reproach: If you are innocent and upright, you should not worry; you will not be annihilated. But, if you are being destroyed, then you should worry, because you are certainly not innocent; you must repent and ask for mercy.

Is this way of consoling a friend appropriate? Is the friends' condolence an expression of true friendship? Does their pious preaching reflect basic human kindness? These questions require values-clarification and soul-searching.

The Friends' Rhetoric and Jewish Ethics: When Does Preaching Become Verbal Abuse?

The friends' approach, comforting the sufferer by moralistic preaching, is totally rejected in Jewish ethics. As formulated in rabbinic sources, this approach is insensitive and oppressive. We have no right whatsoever — morally, theologically, or even logically — to tell a person who suffers: "you deserve it" or "your suffering is a divine punishment for your wrongdoing."

A person or a group may adopt such an attitude: "Because of *my* sins, or *our* sins, *I*, or *we*, suffer!" This might be true and even helpful, but one is not allowed to apply such words to others. One must never say to another individual or group: "Because of *your* sins *you* suffer!" Or, about others: "Because of *their* sins, *they* suffer!" This form of misguided theodicy, preached to others, is clearly forbidden in *halakhah* (Jewish law).[6]

We must never say that a person's suffering is retribution, whether directly to the sufferer or indirectly about the sufferer, whether explicitly by pointing an accusing finger, or implicitly by quoting from sacred sources. We must never do to others what Job's friends did to Job.

The friends' poignant rhetoric about the fate of the innocent and the wicked is considered verbal abuse (*ona'at devarim*), proscribed by the Torah verse: "Do not wrong each other."[7] The Talmud says: "This means: Do not hurt each other with abusive words."[8] Elaborating upon this ethical concept, the rabbinic sources point to Job's friends as a negative model:

> For example:
> If your fellow human being
> has been afflicted with disease and suffering,
> or he has buried his children,
> do not say to him words,
> in the manner spoken to Job by his friends:
>> "Remember, please:
>> What innocent person has ever been destroyed?!
>> Where have the upright been annihilated?!"[9]

The friends' preaching — praising God and accusing Job — is condemned in the epilogue as dishonest before God, and by the sages as insensitive to Job. God Himself defines the speeches of the friends as hypocritical, lacking in Jobian honesty (42:7-8): "...for you have not spoken to (or about) Me truthfully (*nekhonah*), as did *My* devotee, Job."

Ironically, Job's protestation against God is approved by Him, though somewhat indirectly (God never gives Job a compliment to his face).[10] In contrast, the friends' adoration of God is straightforwardly rejected by Him. The friends' preaching, depicted in the epilogue as dishonesty before God, is further proscribed by Jewish law as cruelty to people.[11]

The Book of Job and the Quality of Friendship

The Book of Job deals with the precious quality of friendship. The reader of the book is compelled to ask: Were Job's friends kind and loyal to him in his time of need? Were they concerned with alleviating Job's anguish or with pleasing God? How would I have acted in their stead? How would I have reacted in Job's stead? How would I have wanted my friends to support and comfort me? The questions raised by the Book of Job, on the quality of friendship, are as modern as they are universal.

We often get confusing signals from contemporary rabbinic authorities. We are led to believe that there is nothing wrong, morally or theologically, with the method used by Job's friends—that it is religiously correct to explain other people's misfortunes in terms of divine punishment, that it is proper to offer the sufferer spiritual help by preaching religious doctrine. But when this kind of help is offered without adequate sensitivity, how can it not be vicious and hurtful?

Within the context of the book, this appears to be an issue of priorities. Should the friends be more concerned with glorifying God or supporting Job? In the real world, when facing a friend in pain, we feel compelled to offer help. Should we engage in fixing blame or assuaging misery? Should we attempt to vindicate the existing social or natural order, or rather sympathize with the individual sufferer? Whether we use religious or secular terminology, we must, as consolers, be careful not to add guilt to misery. The prophetic and rabbinic position is clear. We must help people. People, not God, need our help. Only by helping people do we truly serve God.

Are Job's Friends God's Devotees?

Job's friends defend God; are they devoted to Him? They urge Job to appeal to God; do they themselves appeal to Him? They are God's staunch supporters; are they also His faithful devotees? They justify God; do they worship Him? They praise Him; do they follow His ways? Ironically, they defend God, though they have no real relationship with Him, and they accuse Job, though they have come to comfort him as friends.

Job has passed his test; he protested God, yet maintained his devotion to Him. Have the friends passed their test? Theirs was twofold — loyalty to Job and devotion to God. When they failed one, they failed the other.[12]

The irony is striking. The friends, who are on "God's side," show no personal relationship with God. They relate to Him as to a remote concept, an abstract idea. Even as the friends defend God, they remain distant from Him. Distant from Job, whom they accuse, they are also distant from God, Whom they defend.

We never hear them praying to God, pleading with Him. It is Job who, at the conclusion of the book, intercedes on their behalf, praying for them to God. But they have never prayed on their own behalf, nor interceded on Job's behalf. They have never pleaded with God to heal Job, to save him from his misery, to restore his fortunes. The friends always talk *about* God, but never *to* God.[13]

At the end, however, God talks to Job's friends through Eliphaz. But not one of them responds to God.

Between God and Job's Friends

God's attitude both to Job and his friends is poignantly revealed in the epilogue, in God's praise of Job and rebuke of the friends, in His address to Eliphaz the Temanite (42:7-8):

I am angry at you and your two friends, for you have not spoken to Me truthfully [*nekhonah*], as has My devotee Job. Now, therefore, take seven bulls and seven sheep and go to My devotee Job and sacrifice a burnt offering for yourselves. And let Job, My devotee, pray for you; for his prayer I will accept not to punish you in disgrace, for you have not spoken to me truthfully [*nekhonah*] as has My devotee Job.

The key word is the Hebrew *nekhonah* (an adverbial noun), which is misleadingly translated as "the truth." More precisely, it should be rendered as truthfully, rightly, properly.

The issue is not whether Job or his friends spoke "the truth" (or "the things which are true") about God, but whether they spoke to Him *in truth* — honestly and not deceitfully.

The lesson: God is more interested in upright people than in upright theology. He prefers people who behave correctly, rather than those who preach correct theology. He delights in a truthful person rather than in a true dogma. God thus confirms Job's warning (in the dialogue [13:7-16]), that "before His presence no '*hanef*' (hypocrite, flatterer) shall come...."

Reproving the friends—"for you have not spoken to/about me (*ely*) truthfully" — God implies: (1) Unlike Job, the friends never spoke *to* God, directly; (2) Unlike Job, they never spoke truthfully *about* God. As if to say: *To* Me, you never spoke at all; and *about* Me, you never spoke in truth.[14]

Job is defined, by God Himself, as "My devotee" (*avdi*). The friends are depicted as theologians. There is a difference between a conception of God and a relationship with God. The former is exemplified by Job's friends, God's doctrinaires—the latter, by Job, God's devotee.

At the conclusion of the Jobian drama, Job is appointed by God Himself as the intercessor for his friends (as were other patriarchs like Abraham and Moses).

What an irony! The friends were supposed to comfort and support Job. They failed.[15] Now Job, the victim, becomes the savior and protector of his friends, shielding them with his prayers from divine wrath.

Why does God tell the friends to go to Job and ask him to pray on their behalf? This gesture is in essence a form of asking forgiveness from Job. The friends thus are saying: "We are sorry." In this way God obliquely tells the friends that they have sinned not only against Him, but against Job as well. Job's prayer on their behalf is indicative of Job's forgiveness.

Job's prayers on his own behalf were also answered by God, but only after he prayed first on behalf of his friends. God listens to human prayer only within the context of human kindness and friendship. In Judaism, the religious and social aspects of worship are intertwined.

Discussion Questions:

1. Speaking to Eliphaz (42:7), God suggested to him that the friends should come to Job and ask him to pray on their behalf. What does all this imply about God? about Job? about the friends?

2. God speaks about Job as "My devotee" — in the prologue to the *satan* (1:8, 2:3), where He describes him as paradigm of virtue, "there is no one like him on earth," and in the epilogue to the friends (42:7), stating that they have not spoken to Him "truthfully (*nekhonah*), as did My devotee Job." God, however, never compliments Job directly, never offers him a kind word, not even an apology. Why? Can you think of a good reason?

3. Do you see value in offering religious support to the sufferer, the mourner? Think of different circumstances and ways of doing it. What would be your guidelines to keep such comforting from turning into moralizing and verbal abuse?

4. Can you see any merit in pointing out to the sufferer a correlation between suffering and past conduct — explaining misery as divine punishment and urging repentance? Can you see instances when this method of consolation is constructive? What do you think of Kushner's (*When Bad Things Happen to Good People* [New York: Schocken, 1981]) theological views and counseling approach? Offer a good defense of the friends in Job. Consider their position, where they come from, also the effect of their consolation on Job.

5. Discuss the effect of silence when consoling a mourner. How do you cope with or react to silence? Is the consoler ever silent? Should one be? Reflect on Ecclesiastes' verse: "A time for silence, a time for speaking" (3:7).

6. Jews read Job in times of sorrow and bereavement. Many of us have experienced or witnessed this custom. What comfort can one derive from reading this book?

7. The friends are on trial by God, as evident from Job 42:7. Are they also on trial by the reader? As the reader, how do you judge them? The very issue of this chapter, "Job's friends on trial," is overlooked in current sources on Job. Can you think of a reason?

Notes

1. Babylonian Talmud, end of *Moed Katan*; Rabbi Yohanan derives this *halakhah* (law) of initial silence at the house of mourning from Job. In *Berakhot* 6b, this silence is considered difficult and therefore the most meritorious aspect of the condolence call.

2. So implies Eliphaz in his first verse to Job, 4:2; Elihu, who refrained much longer from speaking, is even more graphic, 32:18-20.

3. In Hebrew, *ha-ke'ev* (the pain) indicates, in context, abstraction and generality; whereas *ke'evo* (his pain) refers merely to Job's pain.

4. Psalms 37:25.

5. *Rashi* (*ad loc.*) quoting Babylonian Talmud, *Yebamot* 16a. Surprisingly, the problematic verse (Psalms 37:25) has been incorporated into Ashkenazic liturgy as part of the *Birkat HaMazon* (blessing after meals). How can a sensitive person recite this verse meaningfully in sacred worship? Rabbi Abraham Berliner (Germany, 1833-1915) offers an original interpretation to the psalmist's claim: "I have never seen" (*ve-lo ra'iti*) — watched quietly, approvingly, indifferently, passively — "a righteous person forsaken ..." — and remained uninvolved; for, whenever I confronted such a situation, I would do everything to help and to change it (*Ketavim Nivharim*, volume 1 [Jerusalem: Mossad Harav Kook, 1969], p. 128). The psalmist thus speaks of his consistent, life-long concern and involvement in helping the poor and the needy. Rabbi Berliner's ingenious comment, though far from a cogent exegesis to the verse in context, is an excellent way for the modern worshipper to cope with the verse in liturgy.

6. Moses Maimonides, *Mishneh Torah, Sefer Kinyan, Hilkot Mekhira* (Jerusalem: Mossad Harav Kook, 1955) 14:13, p. 577.

7. Leviticus 25:17.

8. Babylonian Talmud, *Bava Mezia*, 58a.

9. *Ibid.*

10. God speaks about Job's virtues in the prologue to the *satan* (1:8; 2:3), drawing his attention to "My devotee Job," that "there is no one like him on earth," and in the epilogue to Eliphaz (42:7), that "you (plural, all three friends) have not spoken to (or about) Me truthfully, as did My devotee Job." Paradigm of virtue, Job himself never gets from God Himself any compliment or kind word, not even an apology.

11. Babylonian Talmud, *Bava Mezia*, 58a.

12. Both failures of the friends are subtly indicated in two consecutive verses in the epilogue (42:10-11). Their failure as devotees of God is implied by the detail (v. 10), that Job had to pray to God on their behalf, and only his prayer (not theirs) was efficacious. Their failure as comforters of Job is implied in the next verse (v.11), that following Job's restoration, "all his brothers and sisters and all his 'intimates' from before" came to him to break bread at his home, and they "showed their sympathy to him, and comforted him." The three "official" friends are called "*re'im*" (colleagues); the "old" acquaintances are "*meyuda'aw*" — literally those who "knew" him from before. They did precisely what the three came to do but failed. The Hebrew in verse 42:11 parallels verse 2:11. The three colleagues came "*lanud lo u-lenahamo*" but did not; the "ex-intimates" came and did—"*vayanudu lo vayenahamu oto*" — literally, they came to shake their heads in sorrow and sympathy before him (*lo*) and comfort him (*oto*). The Job/friends situation has a parallel in Genesis 20:7, where Abraham prays to God on behalf of Abimelech.

13. The closest to prayer the friends ever get is perhaps Eliphaz's advice to Job (5:8): "If I were you, I would seek God; and to God, I would direct my words...." Meaning: This is what you should do! But Eliphaz was not in Job's condition, and saw no need to seek God. Nor did he offer to intercede on Job's behalf. The irony becomes even sharper when we consider that at the end Eliphaz is compelled (by God) to ask Job to pray for him.

14. The key Hebrew word is "*ely*" — which may yield two meanings: "to Me" and "about Me" — "to Me" as it is spelled (with an *alef*), and "about Me" as a synonym to "*aly*" (with an *ayin*).

15. Their failure is glaring; see *note* 12.

◆ ◆ ◆

Chapter Eight

Job's Recovery As Reflected In His Soliloquies

Job Facing His Past, Present, And Self

Required and Suggested Readings

Text (required):

Third cycle of dialogues (22-26); Job's two soliloquies (27-28; 29-31).

Supplementary Readings (suggested):

Robert Gordis, "The Temptation of Job — Tradition versus Experience in Religion," in *Dimensions*, pp. 74-85.

Hayim Greenberg, "In Dust and Ashes," in *Dimensions*, pp. 217-224.

Archibald MacLeish, "God Has Need of Man," in *Dimensions*, pp. 278-286.

David Wolfers, "Job: The Third Cycle — Dissipating a Mirage, Parts I and II," *Dor le Dor, Our Biblical Heritage*, volume 16, number 4 (summer 1988), pp. 217-226, and volume 17, number 1 (fall 1988), pp. 19-25.

Eva Kahana, Boaz Kahana, Zev Harel, and Tena Rosner, "Coping with Extreme Trauma" in *Human Adaptation to Extreme Stress: From the Holocaust to Vietnam*, edited by John P. Wilson, Zev Harel, and Boaz Kahana (New York: Plenum, 1988), pp. 55-79.

Robert J. Lifton, "Understanding the Traumatized Self: Imagery, Symbolization and Transformation" in *Human Adaptation to Extreme Stress: From the Holocaust to Vietnam*, edited by John P. Wilson, Zev Harel, and Boaz Kahana (New York: Plenum, 1988), pp. 7-31.

Choosing Life:
Job's Evolving Attitude to Life and Death

Job's recovery is illustrated by his emergence from despair to hope as he overcomes his depression and looks with resolve to a better future.

Choosing life is at the core of Job's recovery. In his early speeches he expresses resentment toward life and enchantment with death. Bursting forth from his silence, Job erupts into a tirade. He curses the day and night of his birth, while he adores the grave (*sheol*); there, in *sheol*, one finds tranquility and social equality and no oppression (3:13; 3:17-19).

This yearning for death as an escape from misery sets the tone for Job's responses throughout the first cycle of the dialogue (3-14).

At the close of the first cycle, Job begins to hint at his reservations. Death, idyllic as it first appears, is not his ideal. Job still dreams of the grave as his only available shelter, but sees it as a haven for a while, not a home forever. *Sheol* is an asylum, not a domicile. He wants to visit there, not to live there forever. Job begins to entertain a novel wish to remain alive in the grave temporarily, as a fugitive, a transient guest, not as a resident (14:13-14):

> Would that You hide me in *sheol*,
> Keep me sheltered there —
> Until Your fury is gone....

Job knows this is an impossible dream (14:7-12). A wilting tree has *tikvah* (hope),[1] but a dead man — does not. A tree, though cut down, can still renew itself, but a human being can never be revived from the sleep of death. Job still clings to his previous death wish; he yearns for the grave, though only to hide there. In the second cycle of the dialogue Job begins to harbor second thoughts.

This dramatic change of heart occurs in Job's very next speech, his first in the second cycle. There, Job abandons his death wish and looks for his *tikvah*.[2] The grave offers him none (17:13-16):

If I hope (*akaveh*) for the grave (*sheol*) to be my home —
to make my bed in the dark;
to call the pit "my father";
and the maggots "my mother," "my sister" —
Where, then, is my *tikvah*?
And who can see my *tikvah*?
Will my *tikvah*, too, go down to the grave?
Shall we both (I and my *tikvah*) rest together in the dust?

Job realizes that his wish, anticipating the shelter of the grave, is a nightmare. He shudders as he contrasts this elusive, surrealistic *tikvah* with the vital, realistic *tikvah* of the withered tree (14:7). Job will now continue his search for his *tikvah* — his connecting cord to life — within life's domain.

But only after the dialogues are over does Job express his wish to live in positive terms. Job discloses his innate lust for life, for the first time, in his nostalgic soliloquy, as he recollects his earlier, pre-trial life (29). He celebrates life by yearning for its restoration (29:2-3):

I wish I were as in bygone days,
When God watched over me;
When His lamp shone above my head,
By His light I walked through the darkness!

Recovery as Rediscovery of Self:
Job's Evolving Mood From Despair to Hope

Job's recovery lies in his rediscovery of self. His desperate mood, dominating the dialogue, is powerfully articulated in his responses to his friends. But, as he confronts the chill of their words, the gradual process of self-healing begins. The final stages of this process, leading to Job's rediscovery of self, are sharply depicted in the five chapters which make up his two soliloquies (27-28 and 29-31).

Job, in his first soliloquy, reflects on divine justice (27) and divine wisdom (28). In his second soliloquy, Job contemplates his past (29) and present (30), lamenting his fall from glory to shame, and in a pensive mood, at times lyrical and solemn, Job asserts his innocence (31). The three units of this soliloquy are entwined. In contrast to his fortunes, that have changed from success (29) to degradation (30), his virtues have remained unchanged from his blissful past to his miserable present (31).

The change in Job's mood from despair to recovery is dramatized by the sudden transition from dialogue to soliloquy — from reacting to others, to turning inwardly toward self. This critical transformation is seen in both the hero's disposition and the book's composition.

From his final dialogical speech (26), through his lengthy soliloquies (27-31), to the climactic conclusion (31:40), Job speaks without a pause. The reader wonders: Why do Job's dialogues end and his soliloquies begin?

From Dialogue to Soliloquy

Bildad, in his third cycle speech (25), has shown that he has nothing new to say. His speech is brusque and hollow; it repeats Eliphaz's platitudes (4:18-19) almost verbatim, as well as some of Job's earlier words (9:2). The last cycle thus goes all the way back to the first — from wishing for death to dreading death, from rejecting life to affirming life. The complete round of dialogue in the Book of Job has now come to its close. Before the third cycle is completed, the dialogue fails and fades in disarray.

This unexpected abruptness, dramatically displayed by the "unsymmetrical" text, is crucial. The sudden evanescence is bewildering, yet eye-opening. The reader, if attuned to the book's own pulsating rhythm, will realize that the lack of symmetry at the conclusion of the dialogue is not a literary flaw but an asset. The rupture in design is purposeful and effective. It illustrates the failure and collapse of the dialogue. The friends have exhausted all their arguments. They now disappear from the scene, as their words vanish in the mist of frustration.

Job's final reply (26), appropriately, ridicules Bildad's impotence and mocks the shallowness of his ideas. It opens with derisive, interrogatory monosyllables, "What?" "Whose?" "*mah*?" "*mee*?" (26:2-4):[3]

> "*mah*" lines:
>> What (*mah*) help can you offer —
>>> without strength?!
>> [*What (mah) help can you*] deliver —
>>> with a powerless arm?!
>> What (*mah*) advice do you give —
>>> without wisdom?!
>> [*What (mah)*] counsel [*do you*] so profusely proclaim —
>>> [*without wisdom?!*]
> "*mee*" lines:
>> Whose (*mee*) are the words you utter?!
>> Whose (*mee*) is the breath issued from you?!

Job, following these triumphant *mah* and *mee* verses, continues with a portrayal of God's awesome might in both the natural and mythological orders (26:5-14). Job's adoration of God, which comes as a surprise, is cast in sarcasm. It contrasts God's power and the friends' feebleness. In a final, sweeping verse, which invokes the "what?" and "who?" sounds, *mah* and *mee*, of the opening verses, Job's mockery at the friends' presumptuousness is rekindled (26:14):

> Yes, these are but glimpses of His ways:
> And what (*mah*) whisper of His word can we hear?
> And the thunder of His mighty deeds,
> Who (*mee*) can comprehend?

Job's affirmation of God's awesome might, at the end of the dialogue, is double-edged. It adores God, while it slights the friends. With the same sweep of sarcasm, Job also shows that if he wants, he too, no less than his friends, can deliver a grandiose adoration of God, confirming Job's initial claim (12:3): "I am no less than you...." That Job is awed by God's omnipotence, of which he is so painfully aware, is not surprising. Job is agonized by the eclipse of God's justice. Job now addresses this issue in a new mode of speech, his soliloquies (27).

All dialogue speeches are introduced with a fixed formula: "Then Job" or one of the friends, "replied" (*vaya'an*), indicating a response (*ma'aneh*). In contrast, Job's two soliloquies are introduced differently (27:1; 29:1): "Job continued to deliver his *mashal*" — heralding a new mode of speech. The former are dialogues, the latter monologues. Job continues to speak, but in a different manner. He is not debating but affirming; he is less argumentative and more assertive; he is less combative and more contemplative. Thus begin Job's "*mashal*" soliloquies.

What Are Job's "*Mashal*" Soliloquies?

Chapters 27-31 encompass two soliloquies: the first, of two units (27, 28); the second, of three (29, 30, 31). Each soliloquy begins with the same intriguing introduction, that Job "continued" to deliver his "*mashal*." This means Job continued to speak but not as a respondent. The Hebrew *mashal* refers to a poetic presentation of maxims or parables. *Mishlei*, the opening word of Proverbs (and also the book's Hebrew name), means "Solomon's *mashal* addresses." Within the context of the Book of Job, the term *mashal* defines Job's additional soliloquies which supplement the dialogue. Job's *mashal* orations are distinguished, in mood and content, from his *ma'aneh* responses to his friends. Job's last response (26) leads to his soliloquies (27-31). From here on, Job does not reply but deliberates. Alone on stage, Job speaks to all who will listen.

This drastic break in style, from refutation (*ma'aneh*) to declamation (*mashal*) — following the abrupt cessation of the dialogue — is powerful. Like an unfinished symphony, the dialogue comes to a sudden halt while Job completes his words. After Job's response to Bildad, the reader expects Zophar, the next friend in line, to take his turn on the stage. Where is he? When no one comes forward, Job resumes speaking. The attentive reader grasps at once why Zophar does not appear and why, instead, Job continues to speak. There is no need for the narrator to explain it here. This will be done later, when Elihu is introduced (32:1-3): "The three men ceased answering Job...." Why? Because "they found no answer...."

Job has the last word. The friends are silent; now Job can speak as much and as long as he wants, with no interruption. Thus, in dramatic contrast to his friends, Job will "complete" all his words (31:40).

Job opens his first soliloquy with an oath (27:2-6). He swears by God, the very God Who has "denied" his justice, that as long as he has within himself the breath (and/or spirit) of life (and/or wisdom), the *neshama* and *ruah* which is both human and divine, he — unlike God — will not "deny" his innocence. God has deprived Job of justice, yet Job insists on justice!

This intriguing prelude is crucial. It illustrates Job's perfection in devotion to God, as outlined in the prologue. Job's devotion is unconditional. Job worships God not out of fear or expectation of reward, but out of pure love.[4]

In addition, this oath serves as a compelling introduction to the content of Job's soliloquies, clarifying why Job is no longer interested in arguing with his friends, but rather in presenting his case before God and all humankind.

Structural and Conceptual Design of Job's Final Speeches (chapters 26-31)

Job's final six speeches are: (i) his last reply in the dialogue, to Bildad (26), (ii-iii) his two *mashal* units in the first soliloquy (27-28), (iv-vi) his three *mashal* units in the second (29-31). Thematically linked together, the speeches are presented in sequence, without any interruption, thus comprising one coherent oratorical structure.

Job's final six speeches are an impressive design of symmetry and balance. The first three (26-28)—which include his last reply of the dialogue (26) and his two *mashal* units in the first soliloquy (27-28) — focus on God. The last three (29-31) — all part of the second soliloquy — focus on Job as he turns inwardly, toward self.

The first three chapters (26-28) deal with God and His divine attributes: His unfathomable might (26), His indispensable justice (27), and His unattainable wisdom (28). The last three chapters

(29-31) deal with Job and his human concerns: his glorious past (29), his miserable present (30), and self, as he solemnly declares his unwavering innocence (31).

Whereas in the first three chapters, Job turns devotedly to God, in the latter three, he turns to himself, reexamining both his fate (God's decision) and his integrity (his own decision). This inward turning toward God and self underlines Job's process of self realization.

Job's final orations invoke the opening theme of the book — the link between the two spheres, divine and human. As the prologue projects interlocking scenes of Heaven and Earth, so do Job's final orations.

Table 2:
Job's Final Six Chapters

Chapter	Theme	Description
On God:		
Twenty Six	Divine Might	unfathomable
Twenty Seven	Divine Justice	indispensable
Twenty Eight	Divine Wisdom	unreachable
On Job:		
Twenty Nine	Job's Past	glorious
Thirty	Job's Present	miserable
Thirty One	Job's Self	innocent

Job's First Soliloquy (chapters 27-28):
Divine Attributes — Justice and Wisdom

Job, pointing to God's limitless might (26) in his final response to his friends, continues to reflect on the idea of God's justice (27). He has the fortitude to expect God's justice, but lacks the wisdom to comprehend it. This leads to the exquisite hymn on Wisdom (28). Wisdom (*hokhmah*, featured as a feminine figure) is precious and elusive. Job marvels at her sublime mystery.

Job's Hymn to Wisdom (28) — part two of Job's first soliloquy (27-28) — describes Wisdom's divine origin and manifestations in lucid verses. Its seminal thesis is that Wisdom can never be acquired by mortals. As much as we are endowed with the intelligence to utilize nature for our benefit, we still do not truly possess Wisdom. Our cultivation of the earth and our ability to ferret out from its depths various precious metals is technical knowledge, not divine Wisdom.

This Wisdom, by which God rules His universe — the key to deciphering the mystery of human suffering and divine justice (the Jobian mystery) — remains forever hidden.

As much as we search for Wisdom, we can never find it. God alone knows its origin and meaning. To humankind (*adam*), God revealed a spark of His Wisdom, in the form of religio-ethical ideals (28:28), namely, living a life of devotion to God (*yirat hashem*) and rejection of evil (*sur mera*). This is the only Wisdom accessible to all of us. This spark of Wisdom — edifying us to perform pious and moral acts in adherence to God's Will — is revealed, but the Wisdom of God's Will in His rule over the universe is hidden. Who can find it?

Job's view on Wisdom is better appreciated when we compare it to the other Wisdom books, Proverbs and Ecclesiastes. All three biblical Wisdom books recognize three basic qualities in Wisdom: divinity, usefulness, and mystery. Each of the Wisdom books, however, mentions only two of the Wisdom qualities. Proverbs acknowledges Wisdom's divine origin and worldly benefits, but ignores her elusiveness — Wisdom (female persona) is available for all; she even "sings in the streets" to publicize her excellence.[5] Ecclesiastes sees in Wisdom both usefulness and mystery (elusiveness, uncertainty, inscrutability), yet ignores Wisdom's divine origin.[6]

Proverbs and Ecclesiastes focus on Wisdom's pragmatic features. In contrast, Job celebrates Wisdom's divine origin and perplexing mystery.

Job's hymn to Wisdom reflects the book's Wisdom roots and background, yet is poetically unparalleled and contextually intriguing. How does Job's hymn relate to the context of the book and to the hero who recites it? How does its theme fit into the book's debate on divine justice and human suffering? And why should an anguished Job, rather than one of the other "know-all" participants, suddenly emerge as the celebrant of Wisdom?[7]

Our text assigns the hymn to Job. The reader is compelled to look for a meaningful relationship between the hero and the hymn. Contemporary critics tend to underscore the hymn's affinity to Proverbs and its incongruity with the Book of Job.[8] But, as demonstrated above, the formal resemblance to Proverbs is rather superficial.

Job's Wisdom hymn, in both spirit and message, is uniquely Jobian and not Proverbian. This hymn, which proclaims divine Wisdom as mysterious, unattainable, and non-utilitarian, could hardly fit within the Book of Proverbs, which insists that Wisdom is useful and accessible.

Job's hymn fittingly appears at the final stage of his recovery. It reflects Job's painful awareness of his human limitations. He is intrinsically unable to comprehend divine Wisdom.

The hymn to Wisdom is a collateral yet eloquent participant in the Jobian argument on divine justice and human misery. The hymn implicitly points to the futility of offering any rational solution to the Jobian problem. God's Wisdom is beyond human reach.[9]

Table 3:
Job's Recovery Chart

	Stage I	Stage II	Stage III
	CRISIS Depression Ordeal of Suffering	**CHALLENGE** Confrontation Ordeal of Theology	**RECOVERY** Realization Coming to Terms With Self
Looking at THE PAST	**FORGETFULNESS** No past; thus no future No memory; no hope 3:24-26	**NEGATION** Past tainted, future doomed Accepting the good as bad	**REMEMBRANCE** Recalling Past Glory Appreciating the good as good Dwelling on positive memories Chapter 29
Looking at THE PRESENT	**INDIFFERENCE** Nothing matters! Despair, surrender, defeat Wallowing in present misery 7:16	**RESIGNATION** Man is helpless Submission to God Accepting the bad as good	**FACING REALITY** Transcending present agony Protesting God's injustice Rejecting the bad as bad Objecting to the negative Chapter 30
Looking at ONESELF	**INSIGNIFICANCE** "I Failed! So What!" Self-damnation, who cares? 7:20	**SELF-DEPRECATION** Guilt, sinfulness, impurity Self-abuse, to appease God	**SELF-APPRECIATION** Asserting innocence Maintaining integrity! Finding and accepting oneself! Chapter 31

Job's Second Soliloquy (chapters 29-31): Human Concerns—Past Success, Present Misery, and the Obdurate Claim of Innocence

The second soliloquy outlines Job's three concerns in the stage of recovery. Job first recalls his glorious past (29), then laments his miserable present (30), and finally looks at himself, recounting his virtuous conduct before God (31).

The stages of Job's recovery are three: crisis, challenge, and self-realization. He moves from anguish, triggered by loss of family, health and property, to frustration aggravated by his friends' insensitivity, to recovery sustained by faith. The process of Job's recovery is culminated in the following chapters: looking at his past (29), his present (30), and himself (31).

Looking at his past (29): At the first stage of Job's crisis, there is no past. In his initial outburst (3:3-23), only present doom prevails. Job condemns his life in its entirety by cursing the day and night of his birth. At the very beginning, Job claims—in contrast to the prologue's account of his former happiness — that he was never really happy. This mood is expressed in the last three verses of Job's plaint (3:24-26):

> Before my bread, my sigh would come;
> My groans welling forth like water.
> What I feared has overtaken me;
> What I dreaded has come upon me.
> I was never relaxed, composed, rested —
> And now, rage has come.

From the depths of his present misery, Job views his past as dismal. His wealth ("bread") was obtained in sorrow. He was always apprehensive of pending disaster.[10] Job never enjoyed true tranquility. Without good memories of the past, there is no anticipation of a better future — only the comfort and tranquility of the grave (3:13, 3:17).

Scolding his wife, Job is ready to accept the bad and the good from God (2:10), but now he recalls nothing good, and anticipates only the bad. The friends view his past as stained with sin, and thus foresee a grim future unless he repents; they urge him to view his past as morally bad. In recovery (29), Job remembers his glorious past, and is able to appreciate the good as good. Dwelling on bright memories, he can cope positively with his present travails.

Looking at his present (30:1-31:1): At the start of his crisis, as seen in the dialogue's first cycle, Job displays an attitude of indifference to life. Nothing matters! As he wallows in misery, he sinks into despair.

As his anguish becomes unbearable, he finds life abhorent. He prays (7:16): "I had enough! Not forever shall I live! Leave me alone for worthless are my days!" His friends reinforce his sense of futility, encouraging his submission to God. Mortals are helpless; they must accept the bad as good. But Job resists. He rejects his present as bad.

Finally, in the culminating stage of his recovery (30:1-31:l), Job is able to face reality more lucidly. As Job rejects his misery — recognizing the bad as bad — he transcends his agony, and can face, if not accept, his intolerable anguish with renewed hope for an improved future. By refusing to meekly accept his present misery as if it is his deserved lot, Job opens himself to the appreciation of the positive in life and in self.

Looking at himself (31:2-31:40): At the first stage of crisis, Job feels insignificant. He does not yet care to assert his innocence. He does not even mind to admit sin or failure (7:20): "*Hatati*!" I committed *het*, error ("sin"). "I failed! So what! What have I done to You?" Job expresses self-damnation: "Who cares?" The friends intensify this feeling, pushing Job to the brink of self-deprecation, placing upon him the burden of guilt. They humiliate Job in order to please God. But to no avail! God is not pleased and Job is not humiliated.

In the final stage of recovery, as he looks at himself (31:2-31:40), Job reaches the highest level of self-esteem. Now, in a splendid oration, he is able to assert his innocence.

This declaration of innocence is preceded by an intriguing verse (31:1) which requires explanation. In this verse (commonly regarded as the start of the declaration), Job refers to his eyes: "I have made a covenant with my eyes not to gaze on a virgin!" Traditionally, this verse is taken as Job's assertion of chastity. He would never cast a lustful eye, even upon an unmarried maiden. This has a strange ring to it, especially as it precedes Job's claim that he never committed the more extreme sin of adultery (31:9).

In order to understand Job's words, therefore, we must be cognizant of the historical-literary fact (which is a well-kept secret for most Bible readers) that the standard division of biblical books into chapters — which places this problematic verse at the beginning of a chapter — is neither authentic nor Jewish, but medieval and Christian. It is based on speculation. As for our verse (31:l), the traditional dividing line between chapters 30 and 31 must be ignored. The reader is then free to wonder whether Job in this verse declares his extraordinary piety or laments his present misery. It makes more sense to treat the verse as the ending of chapter 30, in which Job bemoans his present state.[11]

At the conclusion of this soliloquy (30:31), Job describes his present condition by bewailing the uselessness of his musical instruments, his harp and flute. Job complains that his harp (*kinor*), prepared for melodies of joy, is now tuned for mourning; his flute (*ugav*), ready for serenading beautiful women (*agov* means romantic courtship), is now used for weeping. Job concludes his elegy (31:l): My eyes, created to behold beauty, are now, tragically, under my restrictive orders (covenant) to refrain from any such beholding (31:1). In my condition, "what for (*mah*) shall I gaze at a virgin?"

Job's utter dejection is the nadir of his misery (30:31-31:l). He is compelled to divert the use of his harp and flute from rejoicing and serenading to lamenting and mourning, and of his eyes from delighting in beauty to commiserating in darkness.

Job's Declaration of Innocence (31:2-40) opens with a solemn oath (31:2-4): "What (*u-mah*) is one's lot from God above...? Is it not calamity for the unrighteous...?" This "*u-mah*" links the opening phrase of Job's assertion of innocence (31:2) and the concluding phrase of his previous speech in which he bemoans his miserable condition (31:1).

Job's final oration reaches a crescendo (31:2-40). It testifies to his high standards of moral conduct. It mirrors his developed sense of himself, as well as his personal moral values. This speech projects the lofty ideals of Hebrew biblical ethics.

When Did Job "Complete" His Words?

This question goes to the heart of the Jobian drama, Job the book and Job the hero: What is the book's ultimate message? What is the hero's final word? At the culmination of Job's final assertion of innocence (end of Job's soliloquies), the narrator adds a short, yet significant, remark (31:40b): "Completed (*tamu*) are Job's words!" But are they really?

This finale is not merely editorial, but is an integral part of the book's narrational and poetic fabric. This terse yet subtle and intricate phrase links Job's soliloquies (27-31) with the rest of the unfolding drama (32:1a). Job's words were "completed" (*tamu*). "Yet (or, thus), the three men ceased (*shav'tu*) from replying to Job." Job's friends (coldly referred to here as "the three men") are now silenced. They vanished from the stage in disarray even before Job began his soliloquies. Now Job's words are so complete (*tam*), that "the three men" are left speechless; *shav'tu* connotes both rest and defeat. Elihu, eager to speak, would not start before Job's words were "completed." But, ironically, now that they are "completed," Elihu will not get a response from Job.

What does "completed" (*tamu*) mean? The Hebrew echoes the narrative's approbation of Job as *tam*, whole. As Job is *tam* — complete, whole, flawless — so are his words complete and full. There is no need for more speeches. Job has told his whole truth, concealing nothing. But are "Job's words" indeed fully concluded? Does he not speak again, as he is compelled to respond to God's voice from the whirlwind (40:3-5; 42:1-6)? Why, then, does the narrator insist that Job has "completed" his words even before this divine encounter?

There is no discrepancy between the narrator's remark at the end of Job's protestation of innocence (31:40b) and Job's reaction in the final revelation scene (38-41). The narrator's pointed finale impels us to distinguish between Job's deliberate speeches, culminating in his eloquent soliloquies, and Job's incoherent utterances before God, which he delivers under the duress of God's overwhelming voice from the whirlwind. Job could ignore Elihu's orations, but not God's.

In concert with the book's design and purpose, "Job's words" were, indeed, "completed" at the end of his soliloquies. This observation must affect our understanding of the real climax of the Book of Job or of Job's moment of truth.

When do we see the final point in Job's experience as projected in the book? Is it, as commonly assumed, at the very end of the book, at the conclusion of God's appearance, when Job, having been assaulted by God's unanswerable riddles, recognizes his worthlessness (as he wallows "in dust and ashes")? Or is it, as the narrator insists (31:40b), at the end of Job's soliloquies — where Job regains his self-esteem?

What is Job's finest hour? Is it at the moment of God's revelation, when he loses himself, or at the end of his soliloquies, when he finds himself? What is the zenith of Job the book? Is it when its hero presumably surrenders to God in total humility or when he faces himself with integrity?

The voice from the whirlwind is staged — at first view — as the book's climactic event, the final solution to Job's agony. Is this really so? Intriguingly, Job has already "completed" his words before his encounter with God. And even as the divine encounter leads to Job's restoration in the epilogue, Job's recovery has already been adumbrated in his soliloquies.

After it has been proven that Job could face himself with respect, he is then ready to face God in the climactic denouement of the book (38-41).

Job's remarkable recovery — from the depths of anguish to the heights of self-appreciation — leads to Job's reconciliation with self, friends, and God. It is the Jobian solution to human suffering.

Discussion Questions:

1. H.L. Ginsberg, in his "Critical Analysis" of Job (Encyclopaedia Judaica, vol. 10, p. 112) perceives the book as a composite of two different stories, one on "Job the Patient" (JP) in the framework and the other on "Job the Impatient" (JIP) in the poem. The two do not

converge. Using Ginsberg's historical-critical method, the reader encounters two unrelated dramas, each about a different hero. Although both characters, the *dramatis personae* as it were, share the same name and endure a similar tragedy, each acts within a different story and exhibits a different personality. The submissive Job of the framework is not the defiant Job of the poem. The former was rewarded by God for his patience; the latter was silenced and rebuked for his impatience. Looking at the Book of Job through Ginsberg's eyes, what are the lessons conveyed by each of the two "unrelated" stories of JP and JIP? Compare these to the lessons conveyed by this guide, where Job is viewed as one book and one hero. Do you sense that Job is one book or two? Does it present one hero or two? Explain.

2. Describe the process of Job's recovery — from patience to impatience, from despair and defiance to reconciliation with self, friends, and God, from despair and anger to inner peace and self-realization. Using "Job's Recovery Chart" (table 3 p. 80) as a general model, find the appropriate verses to illustrate the stages of his recovery and his attitude toward his past, present, and future.

3. Describe Job's virtues as detailed in his innocence speech. Reflect on the reasons he gives for his moral conduct. Construct an "Ethics Manual" based on Job's speech, and compare it with today's concepts and standards of moral conduct.

4. What do you feel about Job's initial suicidal tendencies? Can you relate them to personal experiences of your own or of people close to you? How do Job's expressions on life and death enrich your insight and understanding of people coping with tragedy?

5. Show how Job's lust for life is expressed even as he yearns for death.

6. Discuss the following quote from Rabbi Louis Jacobs, in *A Jewish Theology* (New York: Behrman, 1973), p. 305: "Although the Book of Job is late and although the idea of immortality is strictly relevant to the theme of the book, there is, in fact, no reference to the idea in the book. This almost certainly means that although in the author's day the belief was already widely held, he himself did not share it." Examine Job's notions on resurrection and the hereafter as reflected in 7:21, 14:10, 19:25-26.

7. Job's recovery illustrates a dynamic self-healing process from a traumatic experience. Job is the biblical model for the modern "coping with extreme trauma" — title of a recent article by Eva Kahana, Boaz Kahana, Zev Harel, and Tena Rosner. Job's story may also shed light on the modern quest to "understand the traumatized self," the topic of an article by Robert J. Lifton. Read and discuss these articles (listed in suggested readings for this chapter).

Notes

1. The Hebrew *tikvah* conveys more than hope, which in modern English usage implies a wish or feeling that has a lesser degree of certainty than expectation or anticipation. The English "hope" is milder than *tikvah*; it lacks the force of conviction and resolution with which the Hebrew biblical concept is charged. In biblical usage *tikvah* is related to a line (*kav*), a tangible cord, a flowing current of water (*mikveh*, Jeremiah 14:8). The relation between *tikvah* and *mikveh* (both imply hope and ingathering of flowing water) may account for the imagery of water in Job 14:7-12, as applied to the "hope" of the tree. The Hebrew *tikvah* implies real and concrete spiritual-physical strength, rather than wishful or "hopeful" anticipation. *Tikvah* means vitality, potential of growth, a justified sense of security, leading to a vision of the future forged by the highest degree of faith and self-assurance. Rendering *tikvah* as hope weakens the powerful impact of the original.

2. The Hebrew *tikvati* ("my hope") is repeated twice in 17:5. The idiom *tikvati* appears in Scripture only in Psalms and Job. In Psalms the phrase is identified with God (71:5) and comes from God (62:6). In Job, *tikvati* (6:8; 17:15; 19:10) is provoked by Eliphaz responding to Job (4:6): *tikvatekha* ("your hope"). The term *tikvah* in Job's verses, with or without the possessive (mine or yours), must be understood in its combined "psychosomatic" sense, referring to both Job's spiritual hope for life and his bodily flow (cord or stream) of life (see *note 1*).

3. My English rendition includes, in brackets and italics, the reverberating echoes of the verses, as suggested and enhanced by the rhetoric power of biblical parallelism.

4. According to rabbinic tradition, *Mishnah Sota* 5:5, Job's oath (27:2) proves that he served God out of love and not out of fear.

5. Proverbs 1:20; 3:13-19; 8:1-21; 22-31. The phraseology of Job 28, adoring Wisdom as more precious than rubies (v.18) and asking "where can she be found" (v. 12, v. 20), is similar to the "*Eshet Hayyil*" hymn in Proverbs (31:10-31). Both divine Wisdom (female figure) and the special woman are invaluable; but whereas the latter is rare (but presumably can occasionally be found), the former is altogether beyond human reach.

6. See Ecclesiastes 7:11-12, 9:13-18, 10:2-3 (usefulness); 7:23-24, 8:17 (elusiveness); 9:11, 9:15 (uncertainty).

7. Most critics wonder: Would not Zophar, who is left without his speech in the third cycle, be more suitable for the recital of the Wisdom hymn? Zophar is imbued with the idea of Wisdom's divinity and mystery in ll:6-9, and he could recite the hymn as a way of admonishing Job for daring to "question" God's ways. The prevalent urge to "amend" the text, and assign the hymn to Zophar, is tempting but must be resisted. The text as it is speaks for itself.

8. See, for example, Robert Alter, *The Art of Biblical Poetry* (New York: Basic Books, 1985), p. 92. (His full statement is quoted in *note 9*.)

9. Robert Alter (see *note 8*) claims that Job's Wisdom hymn "is in certain obvious ways cut from different cloth from the rest of the Book of Job. Lexically and stylistically, it sounds more like Proverbs than Job. Its celebration of divine Wisdom does not at all participate in the vehement argument on theodicy into which it is introduced." We take issue; it is our contention that Job's celebration of divine Wisdom does adroitly participate "in the vehement argument on theodicy" and is indeed crucial for the understanding of Job's soliloquies as expressive of his recovery process.

10. As the prologue confirms (1:5), Job was constantly worried about his children's blasphemy in their heart.

11. My interpretation follows A. Kaminka, as quoted by N.H. Tur-Sinai, *The Book of Job: A New Commentary* (Jerusalem: Kiryat Sepher, 1967), p. 435. Unknown to Kaminka and Tur-Sinai, this approach is taken for granted by Rabbi Ovadya Sforno (Italy, 1470-c. 1550) in his *Commentary on Job*, recently reprinted in *Collected Writings* (in Hebrew; Jerusalem: Mossad Harav Kook, 1987), p. 305. Ignoring the Christian chapter divisions, Rabbi Sforno connects 31:1 with the end of the previous chapter where Job laments his miserable condition: "I have even lost my lust for women...." Regrettably, the editor of the 1987 edition of *Commentary on Job* — failing to acknowledge Rabbi Sforno's remarkable insight — "restores" the Christian chapter division to the text, thus marring Sforno's commentary.

◆ ◆ ◆

Chapter Nine

Job and the Holocaust

Required and Suggested Readings

Text (required):

Elihu's speeches (32-37); God and Job's encounter (38:1-42:6).

Supplementary Readings (required):

Elie Wiesel, "A Plea for the Dead" and "The Wandering Jew" in *Legends of Our Time* (New York: Holt, Rinehart and Winston, 1968).

Andre Neher, *The Exile of the Word: From the Silence of the Bible to the Silence of Auschwitz* (Philadelphia: Jewish Publication Society, 1981), pp. 219ff.

Eliezer Berkovits, "God and the Holocaust" in *Faith After the Holocaust* (New York: Ktav, 1973), pp. 67-85.

Supplementary Readings (suggested):

Jean Danielou, "Job: The Mystery of Man and of God," in *Dimensions*, pp. 100-111.

Ernest Renan, "The Cry of the Soul," in *Dimensions*, pp. 111-123.

Where Was God?

The Book of Job describes how a deeply religious man reacts when his faith in God's justice is cruelly tested. Job is victim, survivor, and witness to diabolic destruction. How does he relate to God? Does he curse Him or submit to Him? He neither turns his back on God (wife's position), nor grovels before Him (friends' position), but stands up to Him in protest, demanding justice. Job's drama endures as a symbol of wrestling with God and clinging to faith in times of catastrophe.

Forced to consider the theological implications of the Holocaust, contemporary thought turns to the Book of Job as a focal topic. Our questions are all Jobian:

> Where was God all the time? How could He countenance the infliction of such suffering and degradation on helpless millions, among them untold numbers of innocent children?[1]

Let us consider the views of three of the most prominent writers on this issue: Wiesel, Neher, and Berkovits.

Elie Wiesel

For the Holocaust survivor, Job is an intriguing figure, says Wiesel. In his story "A Plea for the Dead," the survivor explains his relationship with Job:

> I prefer to take my place on the side of Job, who chose questions and not answers, silence and not speeches. Job never understood his own tragedy which, after all, was only that of a man betrayed by God; to be betrayed by one's fellow men is much more serious. Yet, the silence of this man, alone and defeated, lasted for seven days and seven nights; only afterward, when he identified himself with his pain, did he feel he earned the right to question God. Confronted with Job, our silence should extend beyond the centuries to come. And we dare speak on behalf of our knowledge? We dare say: "*I know*"?

This is how and why victims were victims and executioners executioners? We dare interpret the agony and anguish, the self-sacrifice before the faith and the faith itself of six million human beings, all named Job? Who are we to judge them?[2]

In another Wiesel story, "The Wandering Jew," there is a dialogue between a professor and a hobo. The professor, the storyteller, is obsessed with Job. The hobo, a shadow of the *satan*, finds this obsession with Job amusing. The hobo asks the professor: "Tell me what you teach them, your pupils. Let me profit from it, too, won't you?"

> I did not want to, but he insisted. Seized with uneasiness, I could oblige only by mumbling some incoherent sentences about the Book of Job: That tale was in high style then, every survivor of the holocaust could have written it. In my class I spoke of the origin of the dialogue between man and his fellowman. And between God and Satan. I also dealt with the importance attributed to silence as a setting. Then the idea of friendship and justice, and to what extent the one diminishes the other. And the notion of victory in prophetic thought. What is man? Ally of God or simply his toy? His triumph or his fall?[3]

The Holocaust survivor clings to Job and tries to interpret him, which leads to the hobo's mocking cynicism. "Ah well, poor Job," he scoffed, "as if he hadn't already suffered enough without you!" The survivor identifies with Job: "Like Job, I cursed the day I was born, I wanted to die, to disappear, to expunge my shame, to redeem myself."

Andre Neher

Andre Neher elaborates further: "More than the *akedah*, the Book of Job is the breviary of revolt for the man of Auschwitz." Drawing a comparison between Abraham and Job, Neher concludes:

> Abraham never challenged God. He trusted, he accepted.... But Job did challenge God. In the literal text he rose up against God, demanded accounts, insulted and accused Him. One need only repeat his words and gestures in order to know what one should say and do when one is in rebellion against God.[4]

Yet, Job did not persist. At the end, he submitted. Asks Neher:

Why, then, did Job, at a certain moment, submit? Why did he too dive in? Was his pain less intense, his dunghill less foul, his distress less complete because, after too long a silence, God drowned him in a flood of words of which he understood absolutely nothing? And when, at length, his "restoration" took place, could "new" children compensate him for the cruel, absurd, and unmerited loss of his old ones? Did Job not sense that, for all eternity, human memory and language would recall him as the type of the "suffering righteous man" and never as the "righteous man reinstated"? Could he not understand that his final "restitution" was worthless next to his previous suffering, a spurious "happy ending" which could neither be justice nor in logic "make up" for anything whatsoever? Job is truly the biblical rebel who missed the boat.[5]

Professor Neher does not see enough protestation against God in the Book of Job; he would have liked to see more remonstration, more persistence on Job's part. But Neher's profound discomfort with Job's submission to God at the end is based on the traditional perception of Job's final words to God (42:6). Do these words imply submission or self-realization?[6] But even if we assume that Job at the end did not submit, he did, in the epilogue, reach a reconciliation with God. Can we do the same?

The post-Holocaust believer is bent on being more Jobian than Job. Our generations, living after Auschwitz, are inevitably involved in a crisis of faith, unprecedented in scope and magnitude.

There are today too many pious people — including among them Holocaust survivors — who, emulating the proverbial patient Job, fully submit to God. But unlike the literary protesting Job, they ask no questions of God; they either resist their urge to ask, deeming it irreverent, or are content with the traditional answers. On the other hand, many of us face unresolved doubts of an intellectual and emotional nature. Some of us renounce faith altogether, and thus become unable to question God, in whom we do not any more believe. Some of us continue to cling to faith, no matter what, and thus remain unable to desist from questioning God. Ironically, it is a person's inner core of faith that leads him/her to renounce belief in God or to wrestle with it.

Eliezer Berkovits

This concept of "heresy based on faith" is discussed in depth by the contemporary Jewish theologian, now living in Israel, Eliezer Berkovits. In his monumental work, *Faith After the Holocaust*, Berkovits asserts that a believer may lose his or her faith precisely on account of faith. Furthermore he shows that "the 'reasoning' with

God is a need of faith," and thus, "the questioning of God's providence in the death camps was taking place within the classical
tradition of Judaism."

> Only the believer in the living God of Israel is involved in the
> crisis of faith of the death camps; only he can lose his faith on
> account of it. Undoubtedly, for our generation Auschwitz
> represents the supreme crisis of faith. It would be tantamount
> to a spiritual tragedy if it were otherwise. After the Holocaust
> Israel's first religious responsibility is to "reason" with God
> and — if need be — to wrestle with Him.

> The "reasoning" with God is a need of faith; it issues from the
> very heart of faith. When in Elie Wiesel's *Night*, at the hanging
> of the little boy, someone asks: "Where is God now?" it is the
> right question to be asked. Not to ask it would have been
> blasphemy. Faith cannot pass by such horror in silence. Faith,
> because it is trust in God, demands justice of God. It cannot
> countenance that God be involved in injustice and cruelty.[7]

Based on the biblical example of Abraham wrestling with God over
the fate of Sodom and Gomorrah,[8] Berkovits further points out that
"this questioning of God with the very power of faith stands out as a
guidepost at the earliest beginnings of the Jewish way in history."[9]

Drawing the line from Abraham to Job and from Job to the death
camps, Berkovits contrasts the Jobian questioning of God that took
place in the death camps with God's shocking silence: "The questioning of God's providence in the death camps was taking place within
the classical tradition of Judaism." But, what about God?

> Unfortunately, unlike the case of Job, God remained silent to
> the very end of the tragedy and the millions in the concentra-
> tion camps were left alone to shift for themselves in the midst
> of infinite despair.[10]

Berkovits, mentioning the outcome in the Jobian drama, the
denouement of God's enigmatic appearance to Job — and using the
imagery of Job's final reply to God — painfully concludes that God's
shocking silence in the Holocaust overshadows His silence in Job's
drama.

In Job's drama, God finally revealed himself to the sufferer.

> No such denouement to the drama of faith took place in the
> camps. To the very end God remained silent and in hiding.
> Millions were looking for him — in vain. They had heard of

Him by the hearing of the ear, but what was granted to their eyes to behold was "dust and ashes," into which they — and everything dear to them — were turned.

Berkovits continues:

There were really two Jobs at Auschwitz: the one who belatedly accepted the advice of Job's wife and turned his back on God, and the other who kept his faith to the end, who affirmed it at the very doors of the gas chambers, who was able to walk to his death defiantly singing his "*ani mamin* — I believe." If there were those whose faith was broken in the death camp, there were others who never wavered. If God was not present for many, He was not lost to many more. Those who affirmed and testified to the very end did so in authentic faith.[11]

Berkovits proceeds to draw a comparison between Job and Job's brother:

Neither the authenticity of rebellion nor the authenticity of faith is available to those who are only Job's brother. The outsider, the brother of the martyrs, enters on a confusing heritage. He inherits both the rebellion and the witness of the martyrs: a rebellion not silenced by the witness; a witness not made void by the rebellion. In our generation, Job's brother, if he wishes to be true to his God-given heritage, "reasons" with God in believing rebellion and rebellious belief.[12]

We are all "Job's brothers" — inheriting both belief and rebellion dynamically infused into one heritage. Berkovits, in line with the tenor of the Book of Job, acknowledges the authenticity of rebellion. Steeped in rabbinic tradition, he does so with rare sensitivity.

These are striking lessons from *Faith After The Holocaust*: respect for human suffering, respect for the sufferers—for the victims, the survivors, and the witnesses. Do not accuse those who suffer nor deride those who, as a result of their suffering, display rebellion toward God. To accuse the sufferer, out of one's self-righteousness, is morally wrong. To accuse God, out of one's quest for justice, is morally right.

Discussion Questions:

1. Interview Holocaust survivors. Find out how they relate to the story of Job. In what way does your study of Job contribute to a better understanding of victims and survivors?

2. Reflect on the fundamental differences and the similarities between Job and the Holocaust, and draw conclusions. How does one situation shed light on the other?

3. How do you react to the positions of each of the three writers, Wiesel, Neher, and Berkovits? Whose ideas appeal to you the most, and why?

4. Reflect on the seemingly paradoxical concept of "heresy based on faith." Relate to this concept (explored by Berkovits) by sharing some of your own personal experiences or other events from real life or literature.

5. Job and the Holocaust both raise the problem of human suffering which pervades our very being and continues to trouble us on personal, universal, and many other levels. The issue of suffering — its meaning and purpose, its justification or elimination — has engaged the human mind and heart since the dawn of history. All major religions have been compelled to come to grips with it. See John Bowker, *Problems of Suffering in the Religions of the World* (Cambridge: Cambridge University Press, 1975). The Book of Job is the classic formulation of the Hebraic position on the matter. Human agony is never glorified nor elevated to sanctity (Job at the end emerges out of his "dust and ashes" to prosperity). In Judaism, human misery and evil can never be seen as "a gift to humanity" (compare the Catholic responses to the Holocaust victims' sufferings). Explore and discuss the difference between Judaism and Christianity on this issue.

Notes

1. Eliezer Berkovits, *Faith After the Holocaust* (New York: Ktav, 1973), p. 67.

2. Elie Wiesel, *Legends of Our Time* (New York: Holt, Rinehart and Winston, 1968), p. 181.

3. *Ibid.*, p. 97.

4. Andre Neher, *The Exile of the Word: From the Silence of the Bible to the Silence of Auschwitz* (Philadelphia: Jewish Publication Society, 1981), p. 219.

5. *Ibid.*

6. See chapter 5, "Job on Trial," on "The Vindication of Job: Did Job Finally Repent and Surrender," p. 45; also chapter 8, "Job's Recovery," on "When Did Job 'Complete' His Words," p. 83.

7. *Faith After the Holocaust*, p. 68, 69.

8. Genesis 18:25.

9. *Faith After the Holocaust*, p. 68.

10. *Ibid.*, p. 69.

11. *Ibid.*

12. *Ibid.*

◆ ◆ ◆

Chapter Ten

Lessons from the Book of Job

Required and Suggested Readings

Text (required):

Overall re-reading of the Book of Job.

Supplementary Readings (suggested):

Hans Ehrenberg, "Elihu the Theologian," in *Dimensions*, pp. 93-100.
Leonhard Ragaz, "God Himself is the Answer," in *Dimensions*, pp. 128-131.
Margarete Susman, "God the Creator," in *Dimensions*, pp. 86-92.
Ernest Renan, "The Cry of the Soul," in *Dimensions*, pp. 111-123.
Robert Gordis, "The Temptation of Job — Tradition Versus Experience in Religion" in *Dimensions*, pp. 74-85.
Hayyim Nahman Bialik, "City of Slaughter" (*"Be'ir Ha'haregah"*), in *Selected Poems of Hayyim Nahman Bialik*, edited by Israel Efros (New York: Bloch, 1965), pp. 114-128.
Uri Zvi Greenberg, *"Tahat Shen Maharashtam"* ("Beneath their Plowshare"), *Textures*, vol. 5, no. 4 (June 1987).
Matitiahu Tsevat, *The Meaning of the Book of Job and Other Biblical Studies: Essays on the Literature and Religion of the Hebrew Bible* (New York: Ktav, 1980), pp. 21-26.
Sholem Aleichem, *Tevye the Dairyman and Railroad Stories*, translated from the Yiddish by Hillel Halkin (New York: Schocken, 1987). For a discussion of the Book of Job, see especially the Introduction by Hillel Halkin, pp. xxiv-xxvii.

A Triadic Inquiry

The Book of Job can be viewed from various perspectives: literary, theological, psychological, ethical, to mention a few. Embracing all of them, however, is an educational approach, which stimulates the reader and student to ask: "What have I learned from the book?" The triangle chart will prove helpful in answering the questions raised by the book.

The Triangle Chart

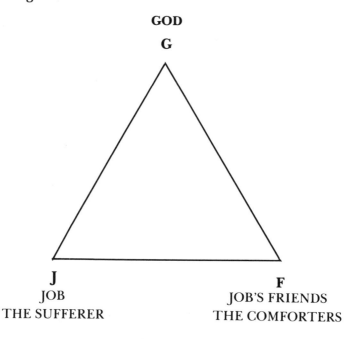

As illustrated in the chart, we shall focus on three themes of inquiry: God — Why does He allow evil to exist? The sufferer — What is the proper response to one's own suffering, in relation to self, God, and friends? The comforters — How should they relate to their suffering friend as well as to God?

God — And the Problem of Theodicy

How do we reconcile the theory of God's justice with the reality of undeserved human misery? This is the overriding problem we encounter in the Book of Job. In modern thought, this theme belongs to theodicy.[1] But, whereas conventional theodicy seeks to justify God, the Book of Job aims to vindicate the sufferer and demand justice from God.

Job's approach is inspired by Hebrew prophecy. The prophets' passion for justice overruled their tendency to justify God. They would never acquiesce to injustice, human or divine. The prophets ask in anguish: Why do the innocent suffer and the wicked prosper? Both Jeremiah and Habakkuk, in their demand of justice from God,[2] follow in the footsteps of Abraham in his protestation against indiscriminate destruction of the innocent together with the wicked: "Shall not the Judge of the whole earth do justice?!"[3]

The underlying premise — adhered to with absolute faith — is that God is indeed a righteous Judge. It is most revealing that Jeremiah prefaces his protestation with a declaration of devotion: "Righteous You are, O Lord; but...." Within the domain of ethical monotheism, there is no other way but to assert God's justice despite contradictory evidence. It is precisely this absolute belief in the ultimate justice of God as a quality which defines His very essence — God is "the Judge of the whole earth" — that renders the problem of theodicy in Judaism so acute.

Moreover, in Judaism the concept of justice is perceived as a human right rather than as a gift from God. A person has the right and duty to demand justice from God, rather than expect it as an act of divine grace.[4] Also, life in this world — in the here and now — is considered sacred. Eschatological responses to the question of theodicy are thus meaningless within the Hebrew biblical outlook, and insufficient even within post-biblical Judaism. Granted that the messianic age will rectify all evils in the future, so what? What about the present? Even the more elaborate concepts in rabbinic Judaism of immortality and a future life in the world to come are inadequate to stem the question of theodicy. How does an eschatological vision — glorious as it may be — solve the problem of God's injustice in this world?

The Book of Job does not solve the problem of theodicy, but it effectively dismisses the conventional answers to it. The most common of them, offered by theologians since antiquity, define human sufferings as: (1) *punitive,* divine punishment for the sufferer's misconduct; (2) *explorative,* divine testing of the sufferer's virtue; (3) *instructive,* divine lessons inspiring the sufferer to improve and return to God.

Punitive: The easiest solution to theodicy — defending God's justice by pointing to human sin — is rejected in the Book of Job. According to the projection of the prologue, Job's travail is certainly unwarranted. It is not punitive, a retribution for his sins, as his friends claim so heartlessly. The dogma of divine retribution, as an all-encompassing rule, is shattered in the Book of Job.

Explorative: Can God be vindicated by explaining human misery as a divine test of one's virtue? Job's ordeal is projected this way in the prologue, within the context of a fantastic, legendary, celestial setting. Other than that, the Book of Job, remarkably, does not mention this idea, or even hint at it. This perception of suffering as a divine test cannot solve the problem of theodicy. Must God test human virtue by promoting human misery?

Instructive: Let us consider the idea that human suffering entails a divine message and conveys crucial lessons to the sufferer, as advanced by Elihu (33:14-17; 36:8-10). Does this idea help the cause of theodicy? Elihu's elaborate deliberations, spanning four long orations in the Book of Job, are left in splendid isolation and elicit no response. They are simply ignored.

God's revelation to Job, in the book's concluding chapters (38-41), may be seen as concrete evidence for the instructive quality of Job's sufferings.[5] Here God is teaching Job a profound lesson. But what precisely is the content of this lesson? How does it relate to Job's ordeal? And why must God first abuse Job before granting him divine instruction?

Let us see whether these final speeches of God (38-41) are a satisfactory answer to theodicy. They do not deal at all with human suffering nor with divine justice, only with human powerlessness and divine grandeur.

Should this grandeur, manifest in God's creation, dazzle our vision, dull our feelings, and silence our protest as we face the tragedy of powerless victims of injustice who suffer and perish in God's world? Does the world's beauty compensate for its cruelty? Should we allow our aesthetic sense to overpower our ethical sensitivity? According to Robert Gordis:

> The vivid and joyous description of nature in these chapters testifies that nature is more than a mystery; it is a cosmos, a thing of beauty. The force of the analogy is not lost upon Job. Just as there is order and harmony in the natural world, so there is order and meaning in the moral sphere. Man cannot fathom the meaning of the natural order, yet he is aware of its beauty and harmony. Similarly, if he cannot expect to comprehend the moral order, he must believe that there is rationality and justice within it....

The analogy of the natural order gives the believer in God the grounds for facing the mystery with a courage born of faith in the essential rightness of things. What cannot be comprehended through reason must be embraced in love. For the author of Job, as for Judaism always, God is one and indivisible. As nature is instinct with morality, so the moral order is rooted in the natural world.[6]

Gordis, so far, is still within the Judaic theological tradition, particularly as articulated by Martin Buber between the two World Wars (1929-1942).[7] God's justice, as manifested in creation, is all-encompassing; as reflected in human affairs, it is hidden from us. This observation, however, answers neither Job's concern nor the problem of theodicy. Is God's concealment appropriate when the innocent suffer and the wicked prosper?

To Buber's traditional argument that God's justice is intrinsically unknowable by human standards, Gordis adds a new twist, the aesthetic dimension of nature: "nature is more than a mystery; it is a cosmos, a thing of beauty."[8]

Gordis' statement is troubling. To flee from the reality of human pain by steeping oneself in the appreciation of nature's beauty is to step outside the sensitivity of Hebrew Scriptures. Jewish tradition has never succumbed to the pagan temptation of venerating beauty, nor would our sages let beauty blur their quest for justice. Particularly disturbing are Gordis' following lines:

> One other significant contribution to religion emerges from the Book of Job. For the poet, the harmony of the universe is important not only as an idea but as an experience, not only logically but esthetically. When man steeps himself in the beauty of the world his troubles grow petty, not because they are unreal, but because they dissolve within the larger plan, like the tiny dabs of oil in a masterpiece of painting. The beauty of the world becomes an anodyne to man's sufferings.[9]

Gordis' suggestion that "The beauty of the world becomes an anodyne to man's sufferings," is most eloquently rejected by Matitiahu Tsevat:

> If the question is justice, would anyone propose that the demands of justice are met by the administering of an anesthesia to the victim of an unjust sentence? And if the question is pain and torture, the beauty surrounding the tortured may in its contrast intensify the pain.[10]

The question of God's injustice, triggered by human suffering, is not resolved, but enlarged, by the prescribed "anodyne" of nature's beauty. The beauty of nature, as background for atrocity, only accentuates divine indifference to human suffering.

A current theory sees in the mere act of God's revelation to Job a mystical-existential solution to Job's sufferings. Job's experience of "hearing" and "seeing" God (42:5), not the content of His speeches, is the answer. God's nearness heals all human wounds. His majestic presence leads to profound silence; all previous questions vanish when God manifests Himself to the suffering one.

This theory echoes a psalmodic mood. "As for me, God's nearness is [the only] good."[11] But is the intent of God's final revelation to Job to heal him with divine closeness? A profound religious experience perhaps, but how does it explain divine justice in human terms?

The very notion of God first torturing the innocent one, and then compensating him or her with a divine healing experience is shocking. Besides, such an experience may perhaps help the individual sufferer, the chosen one who is the lucky recipient of divine revelation. How does it help the countless sufferers who are not so privileged?

The mythical-existential experience is a personal matter. It offers no cogent solution to the universal problem of human suffering. Even for the sufferer — the one privileged with revelation — his/her experience does not really relate to or solve the problem, but merely ameliorates it. A divine revelation, which does not address the sufferer's agonized condition, can still offer no intelligible reason or purpose for the suffering.

This divine revelation might assuage the pain, but does not endow it with meaning. Furthermore, while new closeness to God dulls the sufferers' sensitivity to their own pain, it might also render them insensitive to the pain of others.

Maimonides on the Book of Job

Let us now turn to the rabbinic view, as expounded by the philosophy of Maimonides. Maimonides offers a rationalistic interpretation of God's revelation to Job. He points out that this revelation "constantly describes natural objects, and nothing else; it describes the elements, meteorological phenomena, and peculiarities of various kinds of living beings" — the sky, the heavens, Orion, Pleiades, the Leviathan, and so on. Maimonides concludes:

> The description of all these things serves to impress on our minds that we are unable to comprehend how these transient creatures come into existence, or to imagine how their natural properties commenced to exist, and that these are not like the

things which we are able to produce. Much less can we compare the manner in which God rules and manages His creatures with the manner in which we rule and manage certain things.

But the term management, when applied to God, has not the same meaning which it has when applied to us; and when we say that He rules His creatures we do not mean that He does the same as we do when we rule over other things. The term "rule" has not the same definition in both cases; it signifies two different notions, which have nothing in common but the name. In the same manner, as there is a difference between works of nature and production of human handicraft, so there is a difference between God's rule, providence, and intention in reference to all natural forces, and our rule, providence, and intention in reference to things which are the object of our rule, providence, and intention.

This lesson is the principal object of the whole Book of Job; it lays down this principle of faith, and recommends us to derive a proof from nature, that we should not fall into the error of imagining His knowledge to be similar to ours, or His intention, providence, and rule similar to ours.[12]

With Maimonides we conclude that God's ways remain a mystery. In the face of calamity, we say with Job (1:21): "God has given, God has taken; let His name be blessed." We acknowledge God's absolute sovereignty, and we accept His judgment. But we dare not presume to understand it.

The Sufferer — and the Quest for Meaning

We cannot understand God, but we can identify with Job. Job—the sufferer — demonstrates the power of the human being to protest God, to demand justice, to seek understanding. Job represents each and every one of us. We are inspired, as individuals, to read of Job's plight and his response to it. Job's response encapsulates what we so often feel yet hesitate to express.

Why did Job react so vehemently? Was it because he was unable to endure the agony? True, his physical pain and emotional distress were unbearable, but there is more in Job's reaction than just uncontrollable rage and anguish. The spiritual force with which Job confronted God, manifest at times in verbal assault, was triggered by his quest for meaning.

Job was hurt because he could not make sense out of his misery. Job turns to God (10:2-3):

Tell me: Why do you torment me?
Does it do You any good to oppress,
That You spurn Your own handiwork?

According to Dr. Viktor Frankl, founder of Logotherapy and author of *Man's Search for Meaning*, the quest for meaning is a universal human trait. In Frankl's view, what threatens contemporary humanity is the alleged meaninglessness of life. Frankl, in *From Death-Camp to Existentialism*, describes his experiences in Auschwitz; reliving that period of his life, he has this to say:

> While the concern of most comrades [the prisoners in the camp] was "Will we survive the camp? For, if not, all of this suffering has no meaning," the question which beset me was, "Has all this suffering a meaning? For, if not, then ultimately there is no meaning to survival...."[13]

Job serves as a classic example of "man's search for meaning." Job is also a noble example of the defiant human spirit.

Because of his courage to confront God, Job was able to recover, which enabled him to encounter God's majestic revelation "out of the whirlwind." Job teaches us how to cope with tragedy, how to face pain with dignity and trust God, but never stop questioning Him.

The Comforters — and the Ethics of Lovingkindness

The Book of Job deals with friendship. How do friends react to and treat a friend who suffers? How do they respond to the sufferer who is enduring a crisis of faith?

The traditional role of friends, in such painful situations, is to share in the sufferer's grief and offer comfort. This should be done with compassion and sensitivity lest it become verbal abuse.[14]

The lesson we may draw from the Book of Job is to avoid sanctimonious advice (exemplified in the dialogue by the friends' speeches) and to practice the ethics of true friendship.

How do we act when a friend suffers? When a friend sits in mourning? We visit. We offer our presence, our readiness to help, to listen. We remain silent, and do not impose on the bereaved individual. We respond to the mourner's words with kind words of condolence, not with sermons on divine retribution and human sin. We are sympathetic, not judgmental. We do not attempt to vindicate God by accusing the sufferer.

The most striking lesson in the Book of Job is perhaps the futility of applying theodicy to the sufferings of others. It is one thing to say: "because of my sins (or our sins), I suffer (or we suffer)." It is another thing altogether to say: "because of your sins, you suffer." The former is critical self-judgment; the latter, hypocritical judgment of others.[15] This form of preaching, which draws a correlation between suffering and wickedness, even when delivered with the best of intentions, is cruel and presumptuous.

A true comforter is one who acts as a friend, not as a preacher. Such a friend will practice lovingkindness rather than preach divine retribution. True solace must reflect human compassion, not religious zeal.

Discussion Questions:

1. What is it that you learned from your study of Job that you did not know before?

2. What are the most memorable phrases in the Book of Job? Which would you want to treasure and quote?

3. Write an essay on your personal lessons from the Book of Job.

4. Based on your experience and on the Jewish people's struggle during the last century, what kind of Job would you have preferred as a role model?

5. Look at Uri Zvi Greenberg's *"Tahat Shen Maharashtam"* ("Beneath their Plowshare"), which appears in *Textures*, vol. 5, no. 4 (June 1987). Discuss the poem in light of this chapter.

6. Y. D. Berkowitz, the son-in-law of Sholem Aleichem, once said of him: "On the table by his bed always lay a small, open Bible that he would read now and then, especially when he had trouble sleeping. I suspected that he was mainly reading the Book of Job, and once indeed, when he began to test me on my knowledge of it, I was astounded by his familiarity with it" (quoted by Hillel Halkin in the Introduction to *Tevye the Dairyman and Railroad Stories* [New York: Schocken, 1987], p. xxiv). Read Halkin's superb translation of *Tevye the Dairyman*, and have someone in your study group review the book. Compare Tevye to Job. Does Tevye suffer as Job does? How does Tevye's arguing with God compare to Job's? Contrast the ending of the Book of Job with that of Sholem Aleichem's *Tevye the Dairyman*.

7. Use the Peanuts cartoon on the next page to foster discussion on the following.

(a) The meaning of suffering and the use of the term suffering in the vernacular:

Charlie Brown considers losing a baseball game as "getting slaughtered again" and asks "what to do" and "why do we have to suffer like this?" How does Charlie's behavior represent, or misrepresent, our own? What kind of suffering do you consider serious and what trivial? Reflect on how grave words ("suffering," "Holocaust," "divine") may lose their significance when used indiscriminately. What

Reprinted by permission of United Features Syndicate, Inc.

do you make of Charlie Brown's final musing about his team becoming a theological seminary? Why is a discussion on human suffering (even when it doesn't mention God) considered theological? The Book of Job, unlike the cartoon, relates to God. Is the book, in your opinion, about theology?

(b) Job's friends and their view of human destiny:

The friends' preaching that mortals are destined to trouble is quoted by Schroeder in response to Charlie Brown's grumbling. Check the verse in context (5:7; Eliphaz's first speech), compare translations, and reach your own understanding of the verse's meaning. What does Schroeder think about the value of human suffering? And Pigpen about its inevitability? And Lucy about its indication of human fault? (Distinguish between Lucy's opinion and her attitude.)

Examine the characters' phrases, compare them with Jobian verses, and react.

(c) The advice of Job's wife:

Do you agree with Lucy that she doesn't get enough credit? Of all the cartoon's figures, it is the girl who speaks up for a woman, and gets no reaction from the boys. How does this reflect your experience?

(d) The patience of Job:

What does Linus (who knows the Book of Job by chapter and verse) say about Job's patience? What do you learn about it from this guide? What do you conclude?

What is your opinion on producing cartoons related to biblical themes and on using them in biblical study?

8. Compare your previous notes on your impressions and expectations from the study of Job with your present feelings about the book. Draw conclusions from this comparison.

9. Write your evaluation and/or criticism of this education guide and its approach. Points for consideration: What do you think of the Triangle of Trials concept as a literary insight and/or methodological device? Reflect on the idea of the reader's active role, on the moral lessons, on coping with one's own sufferings and the sufferings of others, on relating to the sufferer, on the general approach to Job as a book about human experiences and relationships.

Notes

1. The term theodicy was probably coined by Leibniz (1646-1716). His 1710 work, *Theodicy*, postulates that "God is just." See the conclusion of chapter 3, "What is Theodicy?" p. 32. Also, for other Christian approaches to the issue, see John H. Hick, *Evil and the God of Love* (New York: Harper & Row, 1977, revised edition), and Nelson Pike (ed.), *God and Evil: Readings on the Theological Problem of Evil* (Englewood Cliffs, NJ: Prentice-Hall, 1964).

2. Jeremiah 12:1; Habakkuk 1:13.

3. Genesis 18:25. See chapter 6, p. 45.

4. This idea is implicit in Maimonides' *Guide for the Perplexed* (translation by M. Friedlander [2nd revised edition; New York: Dover, 1956], 3:53, p. 392-393). Maimonides shows that "the term *hesed* occurs mostly in the sense of showing kindness to those who have no claim to it whatever." In contrast, *zedakah* and *mishpat* both denote "the act of giving every one his due, and of showing kindness to every being according as it deserves." Based on Maimonides, it is remarkable that God is referred to by Abraham as "Judge" (*Shofet*), and by Jeremiah as "Righteous" (*Zaddik*). Demanding justice from God, Abraham and Jeremiah do not turn to Him as "Kind" or "Merciful" (*rav-Hesed*; Exodus 34:6). Jewish to the core, they claim justice from God as a human right, not as a gift from God.

5. Most commentaries on Job, as expected, deal extensively with these crucial chapters. Most Christian commentators (Dhorme, Driver, Habel, Terrien, and others) see in this climactic divine revelation an underlying message to all people to

submit to suffering "as a way of communion with the divine essence of the world." As summarized by Georg Fohrer in his *Das Buch Hiob* (in German, 1963), p. 558: "This is the proper understanding of suffering and man's proper conduct in it: submissive silence flowing from the repose in God." God thus teaches the "impatient" Job to become a "patient" Job; emulating Job, one cleaves to God through one's suffering. Jewish commentators, on the other hand, refrain as a rule from glorifying human suffering or pointing to it as a religious ideal. Our discussion of the revelational chapters (38-41) reflects the latter approach. Maimonides' view will be discussed later in this chapter.

6. Robert Gordis' essay (based on his initial presentation in *The Menorah Journal*, winter 1947) first appeared in *Judaism*, vol. 4, 1955, and is reprinted in *Great Moral Dilemmas in Literature, Past and Present*, by R.M. MacIver (New York: Harper, 1956), pp. 155-178, under the title, "The Conflict of Tradition and Experience — The Book of Job"; and also in Glatzer's *Dimensions*, pp. 74-85, under the title, "The Temptation of Job — Tradition Versus Experience in Religion." It is included in Gordis' definitive work *The Book of God and Man: A Study of Job* (Illinois: University of Chicago Press, 1965), pp. 155 ff. The quotation is from *Dimensions*, pp. 84-85.

7. Buber's "Eclipse of God" theory (together with its literary history) appears in *The Great Ideas Today: 1967* (Encyclopedia Britannica, Inc., 1967), pp. 321-371, as "Additions to the Great Books Library." The core idea is presented in Buber's Hebrew book, *Torat ha-Neviim* (*The Prophetic Faith*) of 1942; the pertinent chapter of which is reprinted in *Dimensions*, under the title, "A God Who Hides His Face" (pp. 56-65).

8. *Dimensions*, p. 84.

9. *Ibid.*, p. 85.

10. Matitiahu Tsevat, *The Meaning of the Book of Job and Other Biblical Studies* (New York: Ktav, 1980), p. 25. Tsevat brings a poignant example from modern Hebrew poetry: "It was just Bialik's sensitivity to a beauty in nature that indeed led him to write in *Be'ir Ha'haregah*, a poem about the pogrom of Kishinev in 1903: '*Ki Kara ...*'" These lines from *Be'ir Ha'haregah* ("The City of Slaughter") — quoted in Tsevat's book in their original Hebrew — read (my translation):

> For God summoned up
> The spring and the slaughter together:
> The sun shone, the tree blossomed,
> and the slayer slew.

For an English translation of the whole poem by Abraham M. Klein, see *Selected Poems of Hayyim Nahman Bialik*, edited by Israel Efros (New York: Bloch, 1965), pp. 114-128.

11. Psalms 73:28.

12. Maimonides, *Guide for the Perplexed*, translation by M. Friedlander (New York: Dover, 1956), 3:22, p. 303.

13. Viktor Frankl, *From Death Camp to Existentialism* (Boston: Beacon Press, 1959), p. 105.

14. See chapter 7 p. 64.

15. *Ibid.*

Supplementary Chapter

Bibliographic Data

I. On The Text Of The Book Of Job

The Book of Job — in its original Hebrew text, or in any of its various English translations, or in both (in a bilingual edition) — is accessible, like any other important biblical book, either (1) in a general, all-inclusive edition of all biblical books, or (2) in a particular, exclusive edition of the book itself.

(1) *The Book of Job in an All-Inclusive Bible Edition*
Although the Book of Job is included in an all-inclusive edition of the Bible, it is helpful to be aware of the difference between Jewish and non-Jewish editions with respect to the placement of the Book of Job. In a Jewish publication of the Hebrew Bible — referred to as *Tanakh* or Holy Scriptures — Job is included in the last (third) division, *Ketuvim* (Writings), following Proverbs and preceding Song of Songs (first of the Five Scrolls). In the traditional Jewish order, Psalms is the first book of Writings, followed by Proverbs, and then Job.

In any non-Jewish publication of the Bible, which includes, as its first part, the Hebrew Bible (so-called Old Testament, OT), Job is placed after all the historical books (which conclude with Esther), preceding Psalms. Job is featured as the first of all the biblical poetical books.

(2) *The Book of Job in an Exclusive Edition*
The Book of Job by itself, in its original or in translation (in its full, unabridged text), is available in a variety of editions, some of them with profound critical commentaries (listed in the Bibliography).

The most popular and useful edition is Soncino's Book of Job (bilingual), with an Introduction and Commentary by Rabbi Dr. Victor E. Reichert. This edition, first published in London in 1948, contains (besides the Masoretic Hebrew text), the English version of the Jewish Publication Society of 1917 (Old JPS). New reprints of this edition are frequently circulated.

For more intensive scholarship and updated insights, it is strongly recommended that you utilize the following modern commentaries on the Book of Job, available in English (see Bibliography): Pope (Anchor Bible, 1958), Tur-Sinai (first edition 1957; revised 1967), Gordis (first edition 1965; revised 1978). These three critical works can be consulted for further clarification of problematic passages. The recent editions of Tur-Sinai and Gordis are bilingual.

The Texts Recommended for Study Sessions

The Soncino edition of The Book of Job, described above, is by far the most suitable text for study. It can be used by all members of the group for both home preparation and class reference. As a supplement, the following bilingual edition is suggested: *Sefer Iyyov: The Book of Job — A New Translation According to the Traditional Hebrew Text* (Philadelphia: Jewish Publication Society, 1980).

This edition contains the *New JPS* English translation, facing the Hebrew Masoretic text. Although it contains no commentary, it is prefaced with introductory material in English by Nahum M. Sarna, Jonas C. Greenfield, and Moshe Greenberg.

Bear in mind that with the concurrent, comparative usage of both editions of the text of Job (Soncino and JPS) — students will have before them both the Old and the New JPS renditions of Job (OJPS of 1917, and NJPS of 1980). This will certainly contribute to a more profound study and appreciation of the Book of Job. As a supplementary textbook, the compilation of readings on Job, *The Dimensions of Job*, edited by Nahum N. Glatzer, is highly recommended. From this text the study leader can assign required readings for each session (as done in this guide).

On the Hebrew Text of Job

Students who read Hebrew are advised to use the original Hebrew text, or have it before them for occasional reference. Two Hebrew texts are recommended. For a critical-textual approach, *The Biblia Hebraica* (by Rudolf Kittel and Paul Kahle; Leipzig, 1929, 1951, and subsequent updated editions) is the most renowned edition of the Hebrew Masoretic text (with a useful critical apparatus). The Koren edition of the Hebrew *Tanakh* (Jerusalem, 1962) is, however, much more suitable for the ordinary reader and student. It is most accurate and more in line with Jewish tradition. Especially helpful is Koren's bilingual edition (known as "The Jerusalem Bible"), which presents in one volume the Hebrew Masoretic text together with an English translation, based on the King James Version (KJV), revised and edited by Harold Fisch (Jerusalem, 1977). Koren's "Jerusalem Bible" is not to be confused with the Catholic Jerusalem Bible in English, a scholarly edition bearing the same name (Jerusalem, 1968).

Two other bilingual editions of the Hebrew Bible are easily obtainable. One is *The Holy Scriptures*, by Alexander Harkavy (1863-1939), who revised the English text of KJV, "in accordance with Jewish tradition and modern biblical scholarship" (from the cover page). This edition was first published in the U.S.A. (New York: Hebrew Publishing Company, 1916; reprints, 1936, 1951). Another bilingual edition — more than a century old, but still very useful — is *The Jewish Family Bible*, by Michael Friedlander (1833-1910), which is an earlier revision of the classic KJV, first published in London by Jews' College in 1881. This edition is now available, in recurrent reprints, in Israel (Tel-Aviv: Sinai Publishing, 1966).

II. On Bibles In English

The popular term English Bibles is a misnomer. There are no English Bibles — only English translations of biblical texts. All English versions of the Jewish Bible, *Tanakh* (referred to by Christians as the Old Testament), are no less and no more than attempts at translation from the original Hebrew, mostly based on the traditional Jewish text — known as *Masoretic* (*Textus Receptus*). All so-called English Bibles are in essence interpretations — each representing a different approach or outlook, a distinct exegetical, critical, literary, or theological point of view.

The English reader is confronted today with a rich assortment of Bible translations. Although at times confusing, this variety has its rewards. Using different versions judiciously may prove very illuminating. It is therefore advisable that more than one translation be consulted for comparative purposes, particularly in cases of difficult verses or problematic passages.

The student should realize that almost all English editions of the Bible — except the Jewish (OJPS and NJPS) — include the New Testament (NT). The Catholic editions also include (as part of the OT) the Apocrypha (Hebrew books composed in Israel during the era of the Second Temple, between the 4th to the 2nd centuries B.C.E.). Books like Judith, Ben-Sira, Maccabees, are not included in the Jewish biblical canon. The two Catholic editions are highly recommended as modern, scholarly translations. Following is a list of some good Bible translations in English, commonly referred to by their abbreviations.

Bibles in English

Jewish:

OJPS (or **JPS**): The Jewish Publication Society version (1917). Since the publication of the new JPS, the old JPS is often referred to as **OJPS**. The OJPS is a slightly modified version of the KJV (mainly in an effort to eliminate and replace the latter's Christological renditions). This translation is available in one volume and also in a bilingual edition in two volumes.

NJPS: The New Jewish Publication Society: Torah (1962, 1967); Prophets [*Neviim*] (1978); Writings [*Ketuvim*] (1982). The NJPS is also available in one volume.

Protestant:

KJV: The King James Version (1611). Known by Protestants as the "Authorized Version."

AS: The American Standard Version (1901).

NAS: The New American Standard Bible (1960).

RSV: The Revised Standard Version (1962).

NEB: The New English Bible (Oxford, 1970).

Catholic:

JB: The Jerusalem Bible (Jerusalem, 1968).

NAB: The New American Bible (1970).

Bibliography

Aleichem, Sholem. *Tevye the Dairyman and the Railroad Stories*. Translation from Yiddish and Introduction by Hillel Halkin. New York: Schocken, 1987.

Alter, Robert. *The Art of Biblical Poetry*. New York: Basic Books, 1985. (See especially chapter 4, "Truth and Poetry in the Book of Job," pp. 85-109.)

Berkovits, Eliezer. *Faith After the Holocaust*. New York: Ktav, 1973.

Berlin, Adele. *Poetics and the Interpretation of Biblical Narrative*. Sheffield: Almond Press, 1983.

Berliner, Abraham. *Ketavim Nivharim (Selected Writings)* vol. 1. Translation from the original German into Hebrew. Jerusalem: Mossad Harav Kook, 1969.

Bialik, Hayyim Nahman. "City of Slaughter" (*"Be'ir Ha'haregah"*). Translation from Hebrew by Abraham M. Klein. In *Selected Poems of Hayyim Nahman Bialik*, pp. 114-128. Israel Efros, ed. New York: Bloch, 1965.

Blake, William. *Illustrations to the Book of Job* (reproduced and reduced facsimile from impressions in the British Museum). London: Gowans & Graye, 1927.

Bowker, John. *Problems of Suffering in the Religions of the World*. Cambridge: Cambridge University Press, 1975.

Breakstone, Raymond, ed. *Job: A Case Study*. New York: Bookman, 1964.

Brenner, Reeve R. *The Faith and Doubt of Holocaust Survivors*. New York: Free Press, 1980.

Buber, Martin. *The Prophetic Faith*. Translation from Hebrew by Carlyle Witton-Davies. New York: Macmillan, 1949.

Buttenwieser, Moses. *The Book of Job*. New York: Macmillan, 1922.

Carstensen, Roger N. *Job: Defense of Honor*. New York and Nashville: Abingdon, 1963.

Crenshaw, James L. *A Whirlpool of Torment: Israelite Traditions of God as an Oppressive Presence*. Overtures to Biblical Theology, vol. 22. Philadelphia: Fortress, 1984.

Crook, Margaret B. *The Cruel God: Job's Search for the Meaning of Suffering*. Boston: Beacon, 1959.

Damon, S. Foster. *Blake's Job*. New York: E.P. Dutton, 1966.

Davidson, A.B. *The Book of Job*. Cambridge: Cambridge University Press, 1937.

Dhorme, Edouard. *A Commentary on the Book of Job*. New York: Thomas Nelson, 1984.

Feuer, Lewis S. "The Book of Job: The Wisdom of Hebraic Stoicism." In *Biblical v. Secular Ethics: The Conflict*. R. Joseph Hoffman and Gerald A. Larue, eds. Buffalo, New York: Prometheus Books, 1988.

Fiedler, Leslie. "Job." In *Congregation: Contemporary Writers Read the Jewish Bible*, pp. 331-345. David Rosenberg, ed. New York: Harcourt, 1987.

Fohrer, Georg. *Das Buch Hiob* (in German). 1963.

Frankl, Viktor E. *From Death-Camp to Existentialism*. Translation from German (1946). Boston: Beacon, 1959.

Frankl, Viktor E. *Man's Search For Meaning*. Revised and updated. Boston: Beacon, 1984. (On the meaning of suffering, see pp. 170-176.)

Freehof, Solomon B. *Book of Job, A Commentary*. New York: Union of American Hebrew Congregations, 1958.

Frost, Robert. *A Masque of Reason*. New York: Holt, 1945.

Gerber, Israel J. *Job on Trial: A Book for Our Time*. Gastonia, North Carolina: E.P. Press, 1982.

Gersonides (Ralbag, Rabbi Levi ben Gershon [1288-1344]). *Commentary of Gersonides on the Book of Job*. Translation from Hebrew by A.L. Lassen. New York: Bloch, 1946.

Ginsberg, H.L. "Critical Analysis" of the Book of Job. Encyclopaedia Judaica, vol. 10, pp. 112-121. New York: Macmillan, 1971.

Ginsberg, H.L. "Job the Patient and Job the Impatient." *Conservative Judaism*, vol. 21, no. 3 (spring 1967), pp. 12-28.

Glatzer, Nahum N., ed. *The Dimensions of Job: A Study and Selected Readings*. New York: Schocken, 1969.

Gordis, Robert. *The Book of God and Man: A Study of Job*. Chicago and London: University of Chicago Press, 1965.

Gordis, Robert. *The Book of Job: Commentary, New Translation and Special Studies*. New York: Jewish Theological Seminary, 1978. (With Hebrew text.)

Greenberg, Moshe. "Job." In *The Literary Guide to the Bible*, pp. 283-304. Robert Alter and Frank Kermode, eds. Cambridge, MA: Harvard University Press, 1987.

Greenberg, Uri Zvi. *"Tahat Shen Maharashtam"* ("Beneath their Plowshare"). *Textures*, vol. 5, no. 4 (June 1987).

Guillaume, A. *Studies in the Book of Job*. Leiden: E.J. Brill, 1968.

Hick, John H. *Evil and the God of Love*. Revised edition. New York: Harper & Row, 1977.

Hone, Ralph E., ed. *The Voice Out of the Whirlwind: The Book of Job*. San Francisco: Chandler, 1960.

Iser, Wolfgang. *The Act of Reading: A Theory of Aesthetic Response*. Baltimore: Johns Hopkins University Press, 1978.

Jacobs, Louis. *A Jewish Theology*. New York: Behrman, 1973.

Jung, Carl G. *Answer to Job*. Translation from German by F.C. Hall. New Jersey: Princeton University Press, 1973.

Kahana, Eva; Kahana, Boaz; Harel, Zev; and Rosner, Tena. "Coping with Extreme Trauma." In *Human Adaptation to Extreme Stress: From the Holocaust to Vietnam*, pp. 55-79. John P. Wilson, Zev Harel, and Boaz Kahana, eds. New York: Plenum, 1988.

Kahn, Jack. *Job's Illness: Loss, Grief and Integration — A Psychological Interpretation*. Oxford/New York: Pergamon, 1975.

Kallen, H. M. *The Book of Job as a Greek Tragedy*. New York: Hill and Wang, 1918.

Kara, Joseph (France, 11th to 12th centuries). *Rabbi Joseph Kara's Commentary on Job* (Hebrew). Moshe M. Ahrend, ed. Jerusalem: Mossad Harav Kook, 1988. (Rabbi Kara, a biblical commentator, was a colleague and student of Rashi.)

Kaufmann, Yehezkel. *Religion of Israel*. Translation from Hebrew by Moshe Greenberg. Illinois: University of Chicago Press, 1960.

Kraeling, E.G. *The Book of the Ways of God*. New York: Scribner's, 1939.

Kurzweil, B. "Job and the Possibility of Biblical Tragedy." In *Arguments and Doctrines*, pp. 325-344. A. A. Cohen, ed. New York: Harper and Row, 1970.

Kushner, Harold S. *When Bad Things Happen to Good People*. New York: Schocken, 1981.

Lamm, Maurice. *The Jewish Way in Death and Mourning*. New York: Ktav, 1969.

Laytner, Anson. *Arguing With God*. New Jersey: Jason Aronson, 1990.

Lifton, Robert J. "Understanding the Traumatized Self: Imagery, Symbolization and Transformation." In *Human Adaptation to Extreme Stress: From the Holocaust to Vietnam*, pp. 7-31. John P. Wilson, Zev Harel, and Boaz Kahana, eds. New York: Plenum, 1988.

MacLeish, Archibald. *J.B. — A Play in Verse*. Boston: Houghton Mifflin, 1956.

Maimonides, Moses. *Guide for the Perplexed*. 2nd revised edition. Translation from Arabic by M. Friedlander. (First published in London, 1881.) New York: Dover, 1956. (On Job, see 3:22, pp. 298f. For a copy of the original Arabic text with Hebrew translation: *Moreh Hanevukhim*, translation by Yosef Kafah [Jerusalem: Mossad Harav Kook, 1972].)

Maimonides, Moses. *The Code of Maimonides, Book Twelve, The Book of Acquisitions*. Translation from Hebrew by Issac Klein. New Haven: Yale University Press, 1951. (See *Sales* 14:13, p. 57. For Hebrew text:

Mishneh Torah [Jerusalem: Mossad Harav Kook, 1955, reproduction of the Rome edition of 1480] *Sefer Kinyan, Hilkhot Mekhira* 14:13, pp. 577.)

Masnut, Shemuel ben Nissim (Syria, 13th century). *Ma'ayan Gannim ... Al Sefer Iyyov Im Mavo We-Hearot* (Hebrew). S. Buber, ed. Berlin, 1889.

McKnight, Edgar V. *The Bible and the Reader: An Introduction to Literary Criticism.* Philadelphia: Fortress Press, 1985.

Mitchell, Stephen. *The Book of Job: Translated and with an Introduction.* San Francisco: North Point Press, 1987. (Revised edition of *Into the Whirlwind: A Translation of the Book of Job* [New York: Doubleday, 1979]. Neither edition of Mitchell's translation presents the Book of Job in its entirety; many crucial verses have been deleted.)

Naiman, David. *The Book of Job.* Jerusalem: Massada, 1972.

Neher, Andre. *The Exile of the Word: From the Silence of the Bible to the Silence of Auschwitz.* Philadelphia: Jewish Publication Society, 1981.

Pike, Nelson, ed. *God and Evil: Readings on the Theological Problem of Evil.* Englewood Cliffs, NJ: Prentice-Hall, 1964.

Pope, Marvin H. *Job* (The Anchor Bible). Garden City, New York: Doubleday, 1958.

Pritchard, James B., ed. *Ancient Near Eastern Texts.* New Jersey: Princeton University Press, 1955.

Raine, Kathleen. *The Human Face of God: William Blake and the Book of Job.* New York: Thames & Hudson, 1982.

Reichert, Victor E., ed. *Job* ("Soncino Bible"). London: Soncino Press, 1946.

Roiphe, Anne. *A Season for Healing.* New York: Summit Books, 1987.

Rowley, H. H. "The Book of Job and Its Meaning." *Bulletin of the John Rylands Library* (publication of the Manchester University Press), vol. 41, no. 1 (September 1958).

Sanders, Paul S., ed. *Twentieth Century Interpretations of the Book of Job: A Collection of Critical Essays.* Englewood Cliffs, NJ: Prentice-Hall/Spectrum, 1968.

Scharf Kluker, Rivkah. *Satan in the Old Testament.* Evanston, IL: Northwestern University Press, 1967.

Schwarz, I. *Tikwat Enosh* (commentaries on Job, in Hebrew). Berlin: 1862.

Sforno, Ovadya (Italy, c. 15th-16th centuries). *Kitvei Rabbi Ovadya Sforno* (*Collected Writings*, in Hebrew). Jerusalem: Mossad Harav Kook, 1987.

Shapiro, D. S. "The Problem of Evil and the Book of Job." *Judaism*, vol. 5 (1956).

Simon, Neil. *God's Favorite* (a play on Job). New York: Random House, 1975.

Singer, Richard E. *Job's Encounter*. New York: Bookman Associates, 1963.

Snaith, N. H. *The Book of Job — Its Origin and Purpose*. London: SCM Press, 1968.

Sperka, Joshua S. *The Book of Job: Mankind on Trial*. New York: Bloch, 1979.

Suleiman, Susan R., and Crosman, Inge, eds. *The Reader in the Text: Essays on Audience and Interpretation*. New Jersey: Princeton University Press, 1980.

Terrien, Samuel. *Job: Poet of Existence*. Indianapolis and New York: Bobbs-Merrill, 1957.

Tsevat, Matitiahu. *The Meaning of the Book of Job and Other Biblical Studies: Essays on the Literature and Religion of the Hebrew Bible*. New York: Ktav, 1980.

Tur-Sinai, N. H. (H. Torczyner). *The Book of Job: A New Commentary*. Revised edition. Jerusalem, Israel: Kiryat Sepher, 1967. (With Hebrew text.)

Westermann, Claus. *The Structure of the Book of Job*. Philadelphia: Fortress, 1981.

Weiss, Meir. *The Story of Job's Beginning / Job 1-2: A Literary Analysis*. Jerusalem: Magnes Press, The Hebrew University, 1983.

Wiesel, Elie. *Legends of Our Time*. New York: Holt, Rinehart and Winston, 1986.

Wolfers, David. "Elihu: The Provenance and Content of His Speeches." *Dor le Dor, Our Biblical Heritage* (publication of the World Jewish Bible Center), vol. 16, no. 2 (winter 1987/88), pp. 90-98.

Wolfers, David. "Job: The Third Cycle — Dissipating a Mirage, Parts 1 and 2." *Dor le Dor, Our Biblical Heritage* (publication of the World Jewish Bible Center), vol. 16, no. 4 (summer 1988), pp. 217-226; and vol. 17, no. 1 (fall 1988), pp. 19-25.

Afterword

The National Jewish Education Department of Hadassah is dedicated to the furtherance of adult Jewish study in order to help our members and the community live enriched and meaningful Jewish lives.

The Department embarked on its recent mission — study of the Book of Job — at a Brandeis University-Hadassah National Education Seminar in June 1988. The sessions on Job were taught by professor Zvi Yehuda, wise and learned author, who stirred our hearts and primed our thoughts. We are grateful for his painstaking efforts in completing this study guide derived from the seminar. The guide clearly illuminates our understanding of Job, and leads us to grapple with disappointment and loss in our own lives.

The Book of Job ranks among the most profound works of biblical literature, touching every aspect of the human spirit. Its language is powerful, its message complex and enigmatic. Throughout the ages, scholars and students have attempted to explain it, interpret it, and answer the questions inherent in its tale of God's test of man's faith.

Why do the innocent suffer? What is the role of the comforter? Of friends who come to offer advice? How should we view God when in this world innocent human beings so freely suffer — from disease, from disaster, from cruelty and injustice?

Seeking answers to the many questions inherent in Job and its message to us can be a lifelong pursuit. We recommend not only careful study of this guide, but reading from the supplementary resources found in the bibliography. The many and varied texts on Jobian themes, including contemporary commentaries and plays, will surely broaden the vision and understanding of the study group.

It is our hope that through continued exploration of Job's struggle, we too can find ways to overcome the inevitable adversities we encounter in life. In addition, the study of Job serves as an exemplar of how we can argue with God yet survive with faith and strength renewed — as individuals and as a people.

Ruth G. Cole
National Jewish Education
Chair